TODD OUTCALT

THE $5 YOUTH MINISTRY

LOW-COST IDEAS FOR EFFECTIVE MINISTRY

Group

FOREWORD BY
KURT JOHNSTON

The $5 Youth Ministry
Low-Cost Ideas for Effective Ministry

Credits
Author: Todd Outcalt
Executive Developer: Nadim Najm
Chief Creative Officer: Joani Schultz
Assistant Editor: Rob Cunningham
Cover Art Director: Jeff Storm
Designer: Veronica Lucas
Photographer (bio picture of Todd Outcalt): Andrew Attwood
Production Manager: DeAnne Lear

Unless otherwise indicated, all Scripture quotations are taken from the Holy Bible, New Living Translation, copyright © 1996, 2004. Used by permission of Tyndale House Publishers, Inc., Carol Stream, Illinois 60188. All rights reserved.

Library of Congress Cataloging-in-Publication Data

Outcalt, Todd.

  The $5 youth ministry : low cost ideas for effective ministry /
by Todd Outcalt. --1st American pbk. ed. p. cm.
  ISBN978-0-7644-6302-0 (pbk. : alk. paper)
1. Church work with youth.
  I. Title. II. Title: Five dollar youth ministry. BV4447.O775
  2009 259'.23--dc22   2009023053

10 9 8   17 16 15 14 13
Printed in the United States of America.

Table of Contents

Foreword

Every year for the past eight years or so I get together with a group of about 20 other full-time, career-minded youth pastors. We seclude ourselves in a cabin or hotel for a few days and talk about things such as adolescent development, the current and future state of youth ministry, the church's role in culture, and the theological implications of this or that. (We are all very, very smart people.) And while I always find the discussion refreshing and rewarding, I find myself frequently wondering: "OK, this is really good stuff and I'm sure it has some importance, but I need to finish planning a junior high program for this weekend and I could really use some good ideas." Or "So-and-so with his Ph.D. in such and such is really insightful, but I wonder if he's played any really fun games in youth group lately."

I'm thankful for the big-picture, philosophical discussions about youth ministry. To continue being the church that God is calling us to be, we need to think deeply and talk about where youth ministry is headed because much is changing. But the old saying, "The more things change, the more they stay the same," may apply to youth ministry better than anywhere else.

That's why I'm so excited about *The $5 Youth Ministry* and other books like it. Because as much as we need the big-picture conversations, we still need (at least I still need!) people like Todd Outcalt sharing practical, ready-to-use youth ministry ideas. Yep, youth ministry is changing, but it's also staying the same, and one thing that I don't see changing anytime soon is our need for ideas that work. And in the book you now hold in your hands, Todd has provided a boat load of practical ministry ideas that will work in virtually any context.

I have no idea what the size of your youth ministry budget is, or if you even have one! But I'd be willing to bet that it isn't enough.

A financial crisis can be a mixed blessing to the local church. On one hand, attendance tends to increase during tough times; people are hurting and often turn to the church for hope and help. The good news of Jesus Christ becomes really good news when people are in need, and times like these present us with some amazing opportunities. The flipside is that while attendance and receptivity may increase during tough financial times, giving probably drops and most churches try to do more with less. I've talked to youth pastors who've shared slightly different versions of the exact same story: Attendance in their church is strong, and the youth group is growing. But they have been asked to cut their budget. Others have been told to drop their fundraising efforts because in essence, that just "robs Peter to pay Paul." And still other youth pastors must cut their expenses without being given the freedom to reduce programs and services they offer students and their families. What do you do with that? The youth ministry I lead has faced a similar position and this is how I've responded: Pray more, shift the focus from programs to people, and share resources and ideas with other youth pastors.

I don't know how much you paid for this book. If you were smart you "borrowed" it from a fellow youth worker. (Tip: In about a month or two this friend will forget you have the book. That's about the time you write your name in the front cover and it becomes yours.) Whatever the cost, it was worth it. In tough times, spending a little money to save a lot of money makes fiscal sense to me! By writing The $5 Youth Ministry, Todd has provided a great service to us all.

May God prosper your life and your ministry in ways that finances never can.

Kurt Johnston

Introduction

Maybe you've heard this saying: "Tough times don't last, but tough people do." We can probably extend those wise words to congregations and leaders. Tough times don't last, but tough churches do. And so do tough leaders, tough youth directors, and tough youth ministries.

As I write these words, our nation is in the middle of tough times. The news headlines are filled with daily reminders of economic downturns, unemployment, and financial challenges. Many congregations are looking for ways to effectively minister with limited resources. Many youth leaders are searching for creative low-cost or no-cost ministry ideas. And some congregations are simply trying to do more with less.

Of course, how many youth ministries can you name with abundant budgets that allow them to spend liberally even in the best of economic times? I can't name many either. Working with a limited budget is one of those skills they probably didn't teach you in Bible college or seminary, but it's a reality of youth ministry.

Here's another reality: Working with teenagers requires thoughtful creativity. Quality youth workers are always searching for ways to effectively minister to young people. We're constantly hunting for new ideas and helpful tips on saving money, making the most of our resources, and nurturing life-changing ministry with whatever tools, people, and finances God provides.

That's the big idea behind *The $5 Youth Ministry.* In this book you'll find dozens of youth ministry ideas that will help you navigate through budget cuts, financial hardships, and limited resources. At its core, this is a book about giving you tools to build a healthy youth ministry in the midst of any challenge you face, and encouraging your faith and vision to move forward instead of being overcome with fear.

Amazingly, tough times often strengthen our faith. The challenges seem larger. The stakes seem higher. But people persevere and come together. Individually, we rediscover our need for total dependence on God. And as congregations, we find creative solutions to complex challenges.

If you're a youth pastor, I'd encourage you to make this book available to all of your leaders to affirm and support them as they work with students. And it's my hope that leaders in churches large, small, and everywhere in between will discover encouraging concepts in this book that can work for them.

If you're a volunteer leader who received this book from your youth pastor, congratulations! You're working alongside someone with a vision for creatively ministering to teenagers. Keep passing along the ideas and inspiration to others.

The ideas in *The $5 Youth Ministry* can be used in churches and youth ministries of any size, and most of them cost little or nothing. This book delivers some of the best $5-or-less ideas that youth leaders and congregations can tap into—low-cost options that promote high-impact youth ministry. All you need is a heart for Christ, some willing hands, and a desire to help teenagers know how much God loves them!

I hope this book proves beneficial for busy and overwhelmed youth leaders and churches. At the very least, reading this book should spark some creativity and inspiration that will birth new ideas in your youth ministry during tough times.

Don't get discouraged, overwhelmed, or fearful during difficult days. Let's learn from them, and let's make the most of the blessings and resources that God has already given. After all, God's people have always faced challenges—and God has always provided.

A quick note, I encourage you to think through and filter each idea before you use it. If there are any ideas that may be questionable to your students, parents, or church leadership, I'd encourage you not to use them. If you're not sure if it's questionable, talk to your senior pastor or your elder board to get their input before moving forward with the particular idea or activity.

Idea Key

(A) Activity:
An idea that will foster interaction among your teenagers.

(C) Camp/Retreat:
An idea that will work well at off-campus events like a summer camp or retreat.

(F) Food:
An idea that will incorporate food into an activity or help you with meal ideas for your youth ministry.

(G) Game:
An idea that will challenge teams or individuals to compete against each other.

(I) Icebreaker:
An idea that will start a youth service or event with an engaging activity.

(M) Mission/Outreach:
An idea that will give your teenagers a chance to reach out and serve people beyond your church walls.

(S) Support:
An idea that will create additional financial support and resources for your youth ministry or mission effort.

(T) Teaching:
An idea that will encourage teenagers to discover biblical principles through interactive lessons.

(W) Worship:
An idea that will help build your youth worship services and experiences.

Fantastic Five for $5

What is Fantastic Five?

Sprinkled throughout this book, you will find sections of five ideas within a certain area of ministry that we feel are particularly "fantastic."

Topics Include:

$5 Idea Index

As you'll soon see, this book is full of low-cost ideas designed to make an impact on your teenagers. Over the next 14 pages, you'll see all of the ideas in this book listed out, along with some icons representing the category that the particular idea falls into. These icons are explained a bit more in the **"Idea Key"** section (p. 1). Once you find the idea you're interested in, flip to the corresponding page number and you're ready to start your low-cost activity!

$5 Ideas

Animal Kingdom Scavenger Hunt (A)

Big Idea: Invade a pet store in search of God's creation

Supplies Needed: pencils, photocopies of the **"Can You Locate These?" handout (p. 170)**—the scavenger hunt list

Age Level: middle school

Most teenagers love animals, and this activity can be a great idea for a small group. Travel to a local pet store for a scavenger hunt; call ahead and ask the manager or owner if it's OK for your group to do this activity. Before the trip, make photocopies of the scavenger hunt list, and give one to each teenager. Set a time limit on this one. Plan to buy a few fun items before you leave, and distribute them as prizes to the teenagers who get the most points.

Another Kind of Offering

Big Idea: Promote openness to different ways to give

Key Bible Verses: John 3:16-17

Supplies Needed: none

Length: 15 minutes

Age Level: older high school

The giving of our tithes and offerings is a central aspect of our worship of God. Through the centuries, Christians have given financial gifts to build the kingdom of God and to assist the poor, the downtrodden, and the needy. Our giving also supports mission efforts and the work of the church far beyond our individual reach.

But there are other kinds of offerings, too. During a worship service, you could challenge your teenagers to give time or talent. You could encourage your students to serve others through an act of kindness or by helping a neighbor. Teenagers may also respond to challenges about their future and what they can give to others through their zest for life, their energy, or their courage.

Want a daring action for teenagers 16 or older? Challenge them to consider their willingness to be organ donors (which they can indicate on their driver's license). If you challenge your young people this way, reflect upon John 3:16-17.

Ask these questions:

- Have you known anyone who's received an organ donation, or have you known of anyone whose organs have been donated after they died? Share the story.

- How would saving someone's physical life through an organ donation communicate God's love?

- How might being an organ donor provide hope to a person or family?

If you like, invite teenagers to sign an organ donor covenant, and prayerfully ask for God's protection and guidance over the whole group.

Be My Valentine

Big Idea: Express your love through homemade cards

Supplies Needed: card stock, markers, stickers

Age Level: middle school or high school

Here's a fun, easy, and useful activity that will give your teenagers a quick and easy way to create Valentine's Day cards. Purchase $5 worth of card stock, a few markers, and some inexpensive stickers. Distribute the supplies to the teenagers, and invite them to create Valentine's Day cards for their family members and friends.

Big Fling

Big Idea: Make a giant sling to launch water balloons

Supplies Needed: purchased or homemade water-balloon sling

Age Level: middle school or high school

Have an extra $5 lying around the house? (Maybe check under your sofa cushions.) If you have this much expendable cash on hand, purchase or create a giant water-balloon sling. There are dozens of these available online, but you can also create a fling for $5 by visiting a hardware store and picking up the various components. Visit ehow.com to get instructions on how to make a sling for less than $5. Just type in "water balloon sling."

Perhaps you've seen these used at summer camps, retreats, and vacation Bible schools to rousing accolades. Teenagers love to launch water balloons. You'll need adult supervision and some safety measures, but the Big Fling is a cool option for summer fun.

Most slings can launch a balloon more than 100 yards, so you can create some fantastic games with one of these.

For example:

- See which teenager can launch a balloon the farthest. Use a cone or stick to mark the distances.

- Launch balloons toward a group of teenagers who are holding a parachute or king-sized sheet. See if you can hit the target.

- Don't fill the water balloons too full—and see if anyone can catch the water balloons inside a baseball cap. Smaller balloons can be caught without bursting.

- Using chalk dust, make several circles in an open field. Divide the young people into teams. See which team can land water balloons inside these circles. Assign various point totals for the circles.

Blindfold Cupcakes

Big Idea: Attempt to decorate cupcakes with eyes closed

Supplies Needed: cupcakes, decorating ingredients

Age Level: middle school

Ready for a fun snack that will test your teenagers' decorating skills? Try making "blindfold cupcakes." Blindfold your students, and then give each teenager an unfrosted cupcake. Invite the students to ice and decorate their cupcakes using plastic knives. Make sure you have plenty of icing on hand, plus cupcake decorations like sprinkles, candy hearts, and other novelties.

This activity is hilarious to watch! The teenagers must then eat their cupcakes when they're finished. But before everyone eats, vote on the

KEY

Activity	**Games**	**Support**
Camp/Retreats	**Icebreaker**	**Teaching**
Food	**Missions/Outreach**	**Worship**

best, the worst, and the most colorful cupcakes. This event works well on its own or as part of a youth group celebration or holiday event.

Body, Mind, and Spirit Challenge

Big Idea: Involve your teenagers in a healthy eating and exercise challenge

Supplies Needed: photocopies of the **"Body, Mind, and Spirit Score Sheet" handout (p. 171)**

Age Level: middle school or high school

Involve your entire youth group in this fun activity that can have an impact on the whole person: body, mind, and spirit. Teenagers can participate in this challenge as individuals or in groups, and the goal is to become healthier in body, more vibrant in mind, and more spiritually awake.

A month before your Challenge Week, begin promoting the idea to your group. Allow enough time for planning and forming groups, if you choose that option.

Create a brochure or handout that talks about the challenge in an uplifting, positive manner. It's important that you as a leader participate, too. This simple challenge isn't a weight-loss program, a diet, or a gimmick. It's a tool to help your teenagers become more aware of their habits, thoughts, and needs—and have fun doing it. And especially if you're facing a lean time when your youth group food budget may be reduced, you can help the teenagers do more for themselves by becoming aware of their food habits and patterns.

This challenge works well at the beginning of the school year, after Thanksgiving, or even during Holy Week before Easter. You can also create a display board that will keep track of each individual's or group's progress.

When the challenge week is complete, you could award small prizes to the top individual and the top group. A $5 purchase at a dollar store could suffice. Or see if you can get donations for some or all of the prizes. Fitness or therapy centers might donate small pedometers. Clinics might donate health equipment like blood pressure cuffs. And stores might donate a T-shirt, a hat, small exercise equipment, or a pair of athletic shorts.

When you have finished with the challenge, help the teenagers to celebrate their accomplishments. Do your best to make sure everyone feels like a winner.

Boxed Up

Big Idea: Collect boxes for shelters, soup kitchens, and missions

Supplies Needed: used cardboard boxes or paper sacks

Age Level: middle school

Your youth ministry can assist soup kitchens and food pantries by collecting small cardboard boxes. Shelters and food distribution centers often use hundreds of boxes a week.

Boxes used to store photocopy paper, custodial supplies, and books are prime examples of what you can find in your church offices or in the homes of people from your congregation. Remember, you don't have to take food to a food pantry to be helpful.

As an option, if you can't land a supply of cardboard boxes, how about collecting paper sacks from the grocery stores or from people in your congregation? These can often be just as useful as boxes, and shelters, soup kitchens, and food pantries will often scoop them up by the hundreds.

Candles in the Dark

Big Idea: Enhance your worship environment with candles

Key Bible Verses: Matthew 5:14-16; 6:22-23

Supplies Needed: candles

Age Level: middle school or high school

Enhance the mood of your worship services by using candles. If you don't have a stash of candles, visit a dollar store. Most of these stores have large sacks of votive candles for a dollar or less. Keep these on hand to create a worship atmosphere when you need it quickly.

You can try some of the following ideas if you need a jumpstart on adding creativity to your services.

Light of the World
Make a circle of votive candles, and read aloud Matthew 5:14-16 and Matthew 6:22-23. After reading the verses, invite each student to light a votive candle. Pause to reflect on the ways we can be a light in our world.

Send a Light
At the close of a youth gathering, place votive candles on a tabletop, and invite the teenagers to think of family or friends who need prayer. Light a candle as you say each person's name, and remember those individuals in prayer.

Cross Light
As you conclude a youth service, form candles into the shape of a cross on the floor and light them. Dim the lights, and invite the students to gather around the cross and offer prayers. To make Christ's love even more real, invite each student to pick one of the candles and take it home. Remind the students that they are carrying Christ's love and light with them.

Fantastic Five for $5

Fundraising Ideas

The garage sale and the rummage sale aren't the only ideas on the block any more. If you are looking for some unique "sale" ideas, try one of these. They don't require much planning, but they can deliver potentially significant results.

1. Used-Book Sale

A used-book sale usually requires minimal work. Simply set up a few tables, make some signs, invite people in the congregation to bring in their used books, and you're off and running. Many of the same people who donate books will end up buying books from others, so you might not end up with much inventory sitting idle. Sell the used books for a few weeks, and then take the remaining books to a used bookstore and sell them there.

2. E-Bay® Sale

You probably have people in your congregation who've heard of eBay®, but don't know how to buy or sell anything on this popular website. Organizing a youth group eBay® sale is one way to get these folks informed and involved. Some of your teenagers could direct this project or perhaps a few adults who are veterans with the online service. Invite people from your church to bring in items that can be photographed and catalogued. Set up your payment service, post the items on eBay®, and use this to fund youth ministry efforts.

3. Hat and T-Shirt Sale

One of the most fun-filled and funniest fundraisers I've seen was a hat and T-shirt sale. It's a simple concept. Invite people to bring in old caps, hats, and T-shirts (obviously you don't want anything inappropriate). This astounding collection will land you some very fascinating and funny

KEY

 Activity

 Camp/Retreats

(F) **Food**

(G) **Games**

(I) **Icebreaker**

(M) **Missions/Outreach**

 Support

 Teaching

(W) **Worship**

items: Three Stooges T-shirts, chicken caps, fishing hats with lures, funny slogans, and a host of others. Once you get these displayed, sell them or auction them off to the highest bidder. This idea is enormous fun and can net some serious cash.

4. Magazine Trade/Sale

Almost everyone has a few magazines sitting around the house, but many people would love to have more. The magazine racks at local bookstores are always lined with people perusing the shelves, searching for that unique magazine focused on sailboating, home improvement, fly fishing, fitness, antiquing, or some other hobby or interest. Organize a day where people can bring in six magazines and trade these for six others, with a request for a donation to the youth ministry for coordinating the magazine trade event. Or create an event where you ask people to donate magazines, and then charge 25 to 50 cents per magazine. Simply recycle any leftover magazines.

5. Boxed-Gift Sale

This one is fun and exciting. Invite people from the congregation to box up an item from home, wrap it, and bring it to the sale. Auction the various boxes, from smallest to largest. Contents remain secret until the buyer opens the gift at home. Or if you prefer a scream, unwrap the gifts immediately following the purchase. You probably have some good sports in your church who would make this event an evening of pure laughter.

Candy Taste Test (F) (A)

Big Idea: Identify the snack without looking

Supplies Needed: candy bars, knife, paper, pencil

Age Level: middle school

Try this great food and fun event around Valentine's Day or Halloween. Purchase a dozen or more candy bars, cut them into bite-sized pieces, and give each one a number (1, 2, 3, and so on). Divide the teenagers into teams, and see which group can identify the most candy bars from taste alone. A "blind" taste test works best.

As a variation, use a large box of assorted chocolates for the taste test. Keep the "key" to the candy box in your possession (it's usually found on the lid or inside the box), and see which team can correctly identify the most pieces of candy.

Car Interior Cleaning (A) (S)

Big Idea: Take your carwash fundraisers to the next level

Supplies Needed: vacuum cleaners, rags, trash bags

Age Level: high school

Sure, you've held a hundred carwashes, but have you thought about cleaning the inside of the cars, too? Many people will pay to have the interior of their cars vacuumed, rag dusted, and the floorboard trash picked up. The next time you have a carwash, make a few extra dollars by doing the interior work, too.

KEY

(A)	Activity	(G)	Games	(S)	Support
(C)	Camp/Retreats	(I)	Icebreaker	(T)	Teaching
(F)	Food	(M)	Missions/Outreach	(W)	Worship

Card Calendars (T) (A)

Big Idea: Create a month-long devotional tool

Key Bible Verses: 1 Corinthians 12:27

Supplies Needed: index cards, pencils, Bibles, whiteboard

Lesson Length: 60 minutes

Age Level: high school

This highly active learning experience will give your teenagers a devotional resource they can use for an entire month. You will need at least 31 index cards for each member of your group, along with pencils, a Bible, and a whiteboard or display board for writing.

To get started, ask your teenagers to make a card for each day of the following month. Number the cards in the upper left-hand corner (the first card is 1, the second card is 2, and so on). So if you're doing this in August, each student will be making 30 cards for September.

Now using your whiteboard as a display, ask the teenagers to think of specific things they can think about, pray about, or do each day in the coming month that will help them grow closer to God or reveal God's love to other people. On the whiteboard create a list of items for the month. (Examples could include praying for a friend, cleaning up his or her room, reading a psalm, thanking a teacher, helping a friend with a problem, or giving some money to mission work.)

Finally, randomly number these items, and have your teenagers write the corresponding activity on each numbered card. Once everyone has finished this project, each teenager will have a set of cards—one for each day of the month. Every person in the group will then have a stack of cards with a specific topic or activity for each day.

Encourage your teenagers to take their card calendars home and do their best to follow the cards for the entire month. At the end of the month, find out what your teenagers have accomplished and how they've been challenged to grow spiritually and share God's love with others. And because they'll be focused on some common goals, this tool can also help foster accountability among your students.

As you close this lesson, read aloud 1 Corinthians 12:27, and then invite the students to answer these questions:

- In this verse, Paul says we're all part of Christ's body, the church. What is your part, and how well are you fulfilling that role?

- If all of us follow these devotional cards for the entire month, what impact might it have on us as a group of Christ-followers?

Cell Phone Picks

Big Idea: Turn cell phones into tools for learning and fun

Supplies Needed: student cell phones

Age Level: middle school or high school

Most teenagers can send text messages faster than their parents can talk, and the cell phone has become the communication tool of choice for youth. Some youth leaders lament the proliferation of the cell phone. Yes, teenagers use their phones in situations that push the limits of rudeness and social unacceptability. But savvy youth workers can also use the cell phone for a variety of activities and teaching moments—and maybe even teach students some social graces while helping them understand the Bible more clearly.

KEY

 Activity   Games   Support

 Camp/Retreats   Icebreaker   Teaching

 Food   Missions/Outreach   Worship

These activities incorporate cell phones, and each one offers a teaching moment for your teenagers. Add some spice to an otherwise drab meeting or engage your teenagers where they live.

And before you do any of these activities, make sure your cell phone plan either has unlimited texting or enough texts left in your account for the month!

1. Cell Phone Funny Faces

Invite your teenagers to participate in a funny face contest using their cell phone photography feature. Have them send you pictures via text before your meeting (especially if you think you will need to censor any photos), or have them send "live" photos from your youth meeting in a controlled environment, allowing your teenagers the chance to see the photos immediately. Students can vote on the funniest face photo.

This little contest can open the door to some discussion about the use of the cell phone photography feature. Some good questions to ask are:

- When might a cell phone photograph be helpful?

- When might a cell phone photograph be harmful?

- How can we misuse this cell phone feature in social situations?

- Should a Christian use a cell phone's camera any differently than other teenagers? Explain your answer.

2. Cell Phone Random Acts

Hold a contest to see who can snap cell phone photos of teenagers performing random acts of kindness. Invite your teenagers to take their photos one or two weeks ahead of your meeting, and be prepared to look at the various photos that your young people have taken that show their faith in action.

3. Gospel Texting

This idea is fun and meaningful, but you will need to keep this activity to a single text message from each teenager (or you run the risk of overwhelming your phone because of all the incoming text messages). Invite the teenagers to text message their favorite Bible verse (using text message lingo, of course), and then see if the group can "decipher" the messages.

Once you display the favorite Bible verses, discuss them as a group using these quick and easy discussion starters:

- What does this verse tell us about God? About ourselves? About others?

- Why do you think this Bible verse is worth remembering?

4. Can You Do This?

Some cell phones feature enough memory for a brief video. In the youth meeting, divide into smaller teams (one phone per team), and ask each small group to take a few minutes to create a group movement, a human statue, or a funny activity on video. Each small group then shares its video with the larger group, and the other groups can attempt to re-create the movement, statue, or funny activity.

Need examples? How about a video of someone walking on his or her hands? How about two people forming a human pretzel? How about a group doing odd-looking jumping jacks with each teenager using one arm or one leg only? Well, you get the picture!

5. Text Message Reminders

Use text messages to remind your teenagers of important meetings, dates, or gatherings. Make your texts funny and witty. You'll probably get a stronger response from a text message than you will from an e-mail or phone call.

KEY

 Activity

 Camp/Retreats

 Food

Games

Icebreaker

Missions/Outreach

 Support

Teaching

 **Worship**

6. Let's Talk About…

Send text messages to the teenagers in your group about an upcoming meeting. Text the theme of the meeting, and ask the teenagers to come prepared to talk about it. Need possible themes? How about

- World events

- An important school function

- Dating

- Happiness and depression

- The meaning of Easter

7. Clay figures

Have you ever seen a Claymation™ cartoon that uses clay figures that are photographed, slightly repositioned, and then photographed again to form a moving picture? Really cool!

You can do this one using either still pictures or video from your teenagers' cell phones. Give the students an ample supply of modeling clay in different colors, and invite them to make a clay-figure motion picture of a Bible story, or create a movie or infomercial that contains a lesson on spiritual growth.

This project can take a while, but if you allow a couple of group sessions, your teenagers should be able to make a one- to three-minute video. This one is a blast and will be enjoyed by the junior movie producers and directors in your group.

Center Game (G) (i)

Big Idea: Keep moving as you introduce yourself

Supplies Needed: none

Age Level: middle school or high school

This outdoor game will require a large open area such as a lawn or field big enough to hold your entire group, and it's a superb game for a summer camping experience or a retreat. This is a noncompetitive crowd-breaker or introduction game, but it does require the cooperation of the entire group.

Assemble your students in a large circle on the lawn, with a space of 3 to 5 feet between each person.

One person begins the game in the center of the circle. This person says his/her first name while demonstrating a funny movement that also begins with the first letter of his/her name. (For example, "My name is Todd and I like to twirl;" at which point the person in the middle would twirl.) Everyone in the circle must then repeat the person's name and do the movement, too.

Once the person in the middle has completed the introduction and movement, he/she runs to the edge of the circle and introduces himself/herself to another person. That individual then runs to the center and repeats the process. Continue doing this until everyone has been in the center and introduced himself/herself.

For smaller groups, challenge each teenager to do his/her own introduction, plus all the previous people's introductions. You can also make the game move faster by establishing a time limit. This is a fun way to get everyone involved on the first day of the retreat or camp.

Chewing Gum Inventions (A)

Big Idea: Mix different gums to form unique creations

Supplies Needed: $5 assortment of various chewing gum and flavors, disposable food- prep gloves

Age Level: middle school

Your teenagers have their favorite varieties and flavors of gum, but how about giving them the chance to create a new flavor? Divide the group into teams of two or three, with each person wearing a pair of sheer, disposable food prep gloves. Buy at least 12 different flavors of gum, and display your assortment on a table or counter. Ask each team to select no more than five sticks of gum. Then say something like: "I now want you to mix your sticks of gum together and see if you can create a flavor that others might enjoy. After you have completed making your new gum, you need to give it a name. We'll take turns sampling the gums you create."

Allow 10 to 12 minutes for the teenagers to complete their gum manufacturing. Their finished product can be either a ball or a stick of gum; simply cut these into smaller bite-sized pieces for sampling.

After each group has completed the task, invite everyone to sample the new flavors. Some will be quite good. Others will be quite disgusting. Just have fun.

Church Rally Worship (W)

Big Idea: Hit the road to worship God

Supplies Needed: transportation, road rally clues and destination, adult chaperones

Age Level: high school

Perhaps your group has grown accustomed to traveling or spending significant money on worship experiences via concerts, big-name bands, and Christian music festivals. If you're looking for a less expensive way to combine music and travel, try organizing a church rally worship experience.

Setting up a decent road rally will require a bit of time commitment and planning, but it's worth the effort. If you're looking for some quick ideas on how to set up a meaningful road rally for worship, check out the two ideas below.

Head to the Park

Write up a few clues that will ultimately direct your group to the final destination (a local park is usually the best option). The clues should guide your groups of teenagers, driven by adult chaperones, to various points around town where they can discover other clues. (For example, "Look for the largest billboard in town, then turn left across the tracks, and you'll discover a clue on the back of a light pole.") Keep the final destination secret from your teenagers and drivers.

Create enough clues and points around town to keep the rally going for several stops before everyone finds the destination. Again, you'll need time to do this and create the clues, but it's a fun experience. To keep things interesting, release your vehicles in stages so they don't all arrive at the clue at the same time.

KEY

(A) Activity   (G) Games   (S) Support

(C) Camp/Retreats   (I) Icebreaker   (T) Teaching

(F) Food   (M) Missions/Outreach   (W) Worship

Or create two or three routes for the vehicles to follow so they don't attempt to steal clues from the other drivers.

Once the group arrives at the park, have a worship band ready and waiting in a shelter house or covered area for some great worship, or invite a local Christian band to participate in the event.

Head to the Swimming Pool

Looking for a great summertime road rally? Ask a family from your church if the teenagers can hold a pool party at their house. If you choose this option, you can't keep the final destination a total secret because students should either wear or bring along appropriate swim attire and gear. Follow the same concept as the park option, with multiple clues along the way. Set up your destination with a beach worship party theme, with music, snacks, and lots of water and cold soft drinks. The teenagers will love this one, and you don't have to go far or spend much to make it happen.

FANTASTIC FIVE for $5

TEACHING IDEAS

Looking for low-cost ways to teach your teenagers? Need ideas for curriculum? Searching for ready-to-go lessons? Desperate for some quick-hitting and easily accessible resources that you can use once or week-by-week? Try one of these five fantastic ideas that all cost less than $5 to get more out of your teaching time on a smaller budget.

1. Blog It

Search the Internet for blogs that deal with teenage culture, pop culture, or issues affecting teenagers. Print out content from a few of these blogs. Some may actually have questions in their posts that you can use for discussion. And if other people have responded to blog posts with their comments, you can incorporate these, too.

A few good places to begin might include:

- youthministry.com

- morethandodgeball.com

- simplykurt.com

2. Phone-a-Lesson

Think about people in your congregation or community who might be able to speak to your youth with expertise, passion, and concern on a variety of topics. You likely have coaches, school administrators, business executives, nonprofit leaders, or popular personalities in your area who would welcome the opportunity to speak to your teenagers.

As a first step, invite them to speak to your teenagers face-to-face. But if they can't visit in the flesh, consider a Skype™ or iChat conversation. You can find the necessary software online, and it allows you to see the person you are talking to via the Internet. It's a fast easy way to create a lesson.

3. Kid Stuff

Before you pay big bucks for that "going green" kit or hire an expert to discuss teen pregnancy or the rising costs of a college education, why not tap into your own students' wisdom and knowledge? Many of your teenagers are writing top-notch papers, doing research, or creating presentations for their social studies, history, or science classes that could be a perfect learning opportunity for your youth ministry.

Not every teenager can speak effectively to their peers, but some of your juniors and seniors could offer up some quality facts and figures, present an interactive lesson, or even lead a Bible study on a topic that interests them deeply.

Getting your young people involved in this way also creates leaders—and you can always use more of those!

4. Recycle

We can recycle more than just paper, plastic, and glass. We can also recycle ideas and information. Remember that lesson you created five years ago about the meaning of grace? Hey, it's just as pertinent today! How about that series on sexuality? Or the session you led on discovering and using our spiritual gifts? Or that hands-on lesson you conducted in the soup kitchen? Dig it up, dust it off, go forth, and conquer again! Remember: The freshmen who joined your youth ministry five years ago have graduated (we hope!), and you're now looking into the eyes of a different group of young people. They won't know you're recycling. They'll just appreciate all the hard work you put into the lesson.

5. Come and Get It

Get it online, that is! You'll find an amazing array of lessons already designed and written for your use. Some are better than others, of course, and some websites are created one day and disappear the next. But don't shy away from looking for high-quality lessons, ideas, and learning activities online.

youthministry.com

dare2share.org/free

groupmag.com

youthpastor.com

simplyyouthministry.com

pastor2youth.com

thesource4ym.com

Comic Strip Gospel

Big Idea: Dig up some gospel nuggets in comic strips

Key Bible Verses: John 3:16; Galatians 5:14; Philippians 4:8; Colossians 4:5

Supplies Needed: Sunday newspaper comic strips, Bibles, scissors, whiteboard, markers, paper, pencils

Lesson Length: 50 Minutes

Age Level: middle school or high school

Option 1

Assemble a pile of Sunday comic strips (or a sizable collection of newspaper comic strips from any source), Bibles, and scissors. Give each student a section of comics.

You can acquire your stack of comics by asking parents to donate Sunday papers or by visiting a local recycler to see if they have newspapers you could sort; many recyclers will be glad to trade labor for a pile of newspaper comics.

On a whiteboard or projection screen, display one or more of the following Bible verses:

- "For God loved the world so much that he gave his one and only Son, so that everyone who believes in him will not perish but have eternal life" (John 3:16).

- "For the whole law can be summed up in this one command: 'Love your neighbor as yourself'" (Galatians 5:14).

- "And now, dear brothers and sisters, one final thing. Fix your thoughts on what is true, and honorable, and right, and pure, and lovely, and admirable.

- Think about things that are excellent and worthy of praise"
  (Philippians 4:8).

- "Live wisely among those who are not believers, and make the most
  of every opportunity" (Colossians 4:5).

Then say something like: "We sometimes find great truths in humor, and
sometimes even biblical truths and lessons can be found in joy. I'd like
you to pair up with another person in the group and take a few moments
to look at these Bible verses. Then see if you and your partner can find a
comic strip that would illustrate the biblical principle found in one particular
verse. In a few minutes, be prepared to explain why you chose that comic
strip and how it relates to truths in the Bible verse you selected."

Allow 12 to 15 minutes for the teams to choose and cut out a comic strip
and prepare their thoughts. Then go around the group, and ask each pair
to discuss the biblical principle and the comic strip.

Following the lesson, close by reading 1 Timothy 6:11-14 as a prayer.

Option 2
If you're unable to locate comic strips for this lesson, try this second
option. Instead of cutting out comics, have each teenager use markers,
paper, and pencils to create a four-panel comic strip based on one
of the following stories. All of these lend themselves well to a visual
representation of the gospel:

Matthew 4:1-11 (temptations of Jesus)

Matthew 8:5-13 (healing of the centurion's servant)

Matthew 13:1-9 (parable of the sower)

Mark 5:1-20 (demon-possessed man)

Mark 9:2-8 (transfiguration of Jesus)

Luke 15:11-32 (parable of the prodigal)

Luke 19:1-10 (Zacchaeus)

John 3:1-21 (Jesus and Nicodemus)

John 15:1-11 (vine and the branches)

Invite the teenagers to share their gospels with the group, and then close by reading 1 Timothy 6:11-14.

Conduct an Interview

Big Idea: Incorporate testimonies into your worship services

Supplies Needed: a format and list of questions for an interview

Length: 15-30 minutes

Age Level: high school

An interview can become a powerful element to incorporate into a worship service. How about interviewing a cancer survivor, someone who has overcome enormous obstacles or limitations, or perhaps a teenager who has a powerful faith testimony?

You probably have people in your congregation or community who would eagerly give their testimonies in an interview format.

But it's important to rehearse. Don't surprise a guest with questions; follow a predetermined format and list of questions that the interviewee can study. And make the interview concise, even fast-paced—this keeps listeners engaged and leaves them wanting more!

KEY

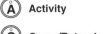 **Activity**   **Games**   **Support**

Camp/Retreats   **Icebreaker**   **Teaching**

 **Food**   **Missions/Outreach**   **Worship**

If you need a few ideas for finding people to interview, consider

- Someone who has a fascinating story of faith

- Someone who is well-known in your area who can effectively articulate an idea or life principle

- Someone with influence in teenagers' lives (such as a head coach, a teacher, or a teenager who has a unique faith story)

- If you're looking for a way to get started, consider using some of these basic questions:

  - What is one thing God has helped you accomplish?

  - What have you learned about being a Christian?

  - What is the most important thing you wish you could tell your friends?

  - How is your faith important to you?

  - Why is your church (or youth group) special to you?

  - What is one life lesson you know today that you wish you had known as a teenager?

Corn Dog Relay

Big Idea: Rediscover the craziness of a corn dog

Supplies Needed: $5 box of corndogs

Age Level: middle school

Yes, corn dogs still exist. And at many wholesale grocery stores, you should be able to find a large box of frozen corn dogs that can be prepared in the microwave.

This food is a relatively inexpensive option for your youth group, and you can combine the corn dog with some fun on a stick. Divide the teenagers into teams, and ask each group to pick a representative to compete in a corn dog eating race. Or if the corn dog simply isn't appetizing enough, organize a corn dog decorating contest. Use mustard and ketchup and see which group can create the most colorful, festive, or "religious" corn dog before you chow down.

And if you want to expand this meal's theme, serve your corn dogs with corn chips and corn on the cob. But be forewarned: Your teenagers may say you're too corny.

Create a Game Ⓖ

Big Idea: Allow teenagers to design their own games

Supplies Needed: cardboard, markers, modeling clay, paints, balls, flags, other random supplies that can be used for homemade games

Age Level: middle school or high school

Teenagers are naturally creative and innovative. If you give them a few items and ask them to create a game out of it, they can. Use this idea in a variety of settings, such as camps, retreats, lock-ins—anywhere. All you'll need is a bag of low-cost items. You can do this as a large group, or you can divide into teams and create several games. Visit your local dollar store for a $5 stash of bargains, and you are off and running.

Some of the games your teenagers create will remain favorites for years to come, and younger teenagers or new students in your youth group will find themselves asking: "Where did this game come from? Who created this?"

KEY

 Activity   **Games**   **Support**

 **Camp/Retreats**   **Icebreaker**   Ⓣ **Teaching**

Ⓕ **Food**   Ⓜ **Missions/Outreach**   Ⓦ **Worship**

Here are some easy ways to create a game.

Create a Board Game

Useful items for your board game kit would include cardboard, poster board, markers, crayons, scrapbook stickers, magazines, newspaper advertisements, scissors, pencils, modeling clay, twist-ties, glue sticks, a ruler, a compass, clear tape, double-sided tape, paper clips, Velcro strips or dots, foam board, wrapping paper, watercolor paints, a set of dice, small tokens, and any other inexpensive items you can pick up from a craft store or craft supply aisle.

Invite the teenagers to create a functional board game complete with rules.

Create an Outdoor Game

Useful items that will help the teenagers create an outdoor game include sport cones (boundary markers), marker flags, an array of various-sized balls, a disk or flying ring, rags that can be torn into strips, gloves, kneepads, netting, goggles, a spray nozzle for a water hose, and any other inexpensive items you can pick up at a used sporting goods store.

Invite the teenagers to create a game that can be played outdoors by a large group, complete with rules and safety regulations.

Create an Indoor Game

Useful items for your indoor game kit might include duct tape, sport cones, small rubber balls, straws, paper cups, table tennis balls, netting, poster board, craft wire, lettering, plastic bowling pins, foam mats, towels, rags that can be torn for blindfolds, goggles, funnels, kneepads, and any other intriguing items you might purchase at a dollar store.

Invite the youth to create an indoor game that can be played safely in a confined space, complete with rules.

You may have trouble imagining a game from these supplies, but don't worry. Your teenagers will come up with something.

Create Bible Bookmarks (S) (A)

Big Idea: Encourage readers and support mission efforts

Supplies Needed: paper, laminating machine, markers

Age Level: middle school or high school

Making and selling bookmarks can become a creative way to raise money for mission projects. Create bookmarks that feature favorite Bible verses, uplifting images, and inspirational sayings. We used a laminating machine to finish the bookmarks in plastic so they had a more professional look. This is an easy fundraiser that will help your mission efforts while providing a practical tool for spiritual growth.

Crock-Pot ® Meals (F) (A)

Big Idea: Use slow cookers to nourish hungry teenagers

Supplies Needed: slow cookers, donated food

Age Level: middle school or high school

Save money on food by enlisting some of the top cooks in your congregation to prepare Crock-Pot® meals or give you some of their favorite recipes. These are easy meals. Drop the ingredients into the Crock-Pot®, walk away, and come back later to a hot meal.

The Crock-Pot® meal is perfect for camping, day-long outings, and summer trips. Prepare the meal in the morning, and when you return at night, the meal is waiting. These meals can also be nutritious and filling, and few teenagers will turn them away.

KEY

(A) Activity	(G) Games	(S) Support
(C) Camp/Retreats	(I) Icebreaker	(T) Teaching
(F) Food	(M) Missions/Outreach	(W) Worship

Desperation Games Ⓖ Ⓒ

Big Idea: Use ordinary objects when you're out of ideas

Supplies Needed: 2-liter bottles, rubber ball, garbage bags, clothing (depending on the specific game)

Age Level: middle school

If you're really desperate for a game—rainy day, no money, plans gone awry—and you have no other choices, here are some quick game options that you can literally pull out of a suitcase or the garbage.

2-Liter Bowling

If you need a quick, makeshift game for an indoor gathering, try 2-liter bowling. Get 10 empty 2-liter bottles (this should be easy). Place these in the traditional 10-pin arrangement, clear a space that can serve as an alley, and then bowl, using a small rubber ball. A wadded-up T-shirt can also work well if you are really desperate!

Garbage Bag Relay

Got a couple of garbage bags? Got a pile or two of smelly clothing the teenagers could bring from home—or dirty clothes sitting in a suitcase after a long trip? Form two teams. One person on each team takes a turn stuffing the bag full of clothing, emptying it, and then handing it off to the next person on the team. Play continues until the last person on one team has successfully stuffed the bag and emptied the clothing at the finish line. A torn bag is grounds for disqualification.

Clothes Sorting

Form two teams. Each team creates a pile of dirty clothing—brought from home or from the trip suitcases. Points are then awarded as follows. See which team earns the most points. (See the point table on next page).

1 Point	2 Points	3 Points
White T-shirt	Blue T-shirt	Purple T-shirt
White tube sock	Green socks	Blue socks
Shirt or blouse	Scarf	Sock hat
Gloves	Mittens	Face mask
Blue jeans	Dress pants	Dress/skirt
Tennis shoes	Dress shoes	Sandals
Ball cap	Panama hat	Belt

Easter People

Big Idea: Take a dramatic look at the message of Easter

Supplies Needed: photocopies of the **"Easter Narrative" handout (p. 172)**, Bible

Length: 30 minutes

Age Level: high school

Not every youth group meets on Easter Sunday, but this idea could help you create a meaningful and moving event for that day or for another meeting during that season. Travel to a local cemetery (sunrise Easter morning or Easter evening works best) and gather your group for this dramatic reading based on Matthew 28. You'll need two people to narrate, and people to read the lines for the Angel, Jesus, and the Priest. This reading is adapted from the New International Version, but you could use any translation you desire. Just use this narrative as a guide.

KEY

(A) Activity (G) Games (S) Support

(C) Camp/Retreats (I) Icebreaker (T) Teaching

(F) Food (M) Missions/Outreach (W) Worship

E-mail or Text a Greeting Ⓢ Ⓐ

Big Idea: Create an e-mail and text message service for your church

Supplies Needed: clipboard, paper, pencils, computer with Internet access

Age Level: high school

Today's technology will let you easily create e-mail and text message greetings. Invite people in your congregation to sign up for this service. Each person should provide the name and e-mail address (or cell phone number) of the person he or she wishes to greet, along with the date to send the greeting. Your teenagers can keep a record of these dates and then send the appropriate greeting to the individual at that time.

Create some simple greetings like these that people can choose from:

Happy Birthday, _____ ! From _____

Thinking of you on your birthday. Love _____

Best wishes on your birthday, from _____

Ask for a $1 donation per message, or allow people to choose the amount they donate to your youth ministry. Create a calendar of the dates and names and numbers, and review regularly. Save some time and confusion by offering this service one month at a time. This can be a great service opportunity for some of your older teenagers or for an adult volunteer looking for a specific way to serve in your youth ministry.

Empty Chair (M)

Big Idea: Encourage your teenagers to invite and unite

Supplies Needed: chair

Length: 10 minutes

Age Level: middle school or high school

This simple illustration can help your students gain a deeper appreciation for outreach and mission efforts. Near the end of your youth service, ask the students to form a circle and place an empty chair in the middle. Then ask:

- Can you think of one person who isn't here tonight that needs a call inviting them to be back with us next week?

- If you were going to invite one person to our youth service next week, who would it be and why?

- Who might God bring into our midst to fill the empty chair next week?

Your students can answer these questions aloud, or you can encourage them to silently reflect on how they would respond. Either way, challenge your teenagers to invite someone to fill the empty chair.

KEY

(A) Activity   (G) Games   (S) Support

(C) Camp/Retreats   (I) Icebreaker   (T) Teaching

(F) Food   (M) Missions/Outreach   (W) Worship

Enlarge Your Ministry (ⓦ)

Big Idea: Launch new student ministry teams

Supplies Needed: none

Age Level: high school

Worship, of course, is far more than music and a message. Worship involves our willingness to enter into a moment with God. It means honoring God with every part of our lives. An effective worship service gives teenagers the opportunity to creatively draw closer to God and honor God in a group setting.

Maybe you have some great ideas for enhancing your services, but your ideas have run into the brick wall called "no finances." You'd like to add more media elements or a new sound system or dynamic lighting effects, but you just don't have the money right now. Consider a different approach: Improve the effectiveness of your worship services by creating or expanding the opportunities for your teenagers to serve.

Add a new ministry team, such as a greeting team, a setup team, or even a signing ministry for the deaf. Organize a drama troupe or a new voice ensemble. Give your teenagers a video camera, and have them create video announcements or an illustrated sermon.

Think of this challenging season as an opportunity to try something new. Be adventuresome in your worship concepts instead of doing the same old thing each week. You'll discover that new approaches, new opportunities to serve, and new leaders bring a zest and renewed energy to your worship services.

Fair Game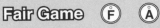

Big Idea: Cook up food you might find at the state fair

Supplies Needed: state fair food and entertainment

Age Level: middle school or high school

State fair cuisine isn't usually considered gourmet, but it always seems to please the crowds. Find inspiration from this summertime tradition, and make your own youth group fair by inviting the teenagers to bring in some of their own food creations: elephant ears, funnel cakes, hot dogs, pickle on a stick, pies, nachos, and so on.

Organize your fair meal around fair entertainment. How about holding a karaoke contest; a yodeling competition; a pie-eating contest?

Invite the teenagers to plan this one. Food and fun in the same package. Low cost but high entertainment.

Fear Factors (T)

Big Idea: Help students address their greatest fears

Key Bible Verses: 1 John 4:13-19

Supplies Needed: Bible, index cards, pencils, photos and images, laptop computer with Internet access

Age Level: middle school or high school

Teenagers are perceptive when it comes to understanding the times in which they live. You probably have teenagers in your church who fear

KEY

(A) Activity   (G) Games   (S) Support

(C) Camp/Retreats   (I) Icebreaker   (T) Teaching

(F) Food   (M) Missions/Outreach   (W) Worship

that a parent will lose a job or that they may have to face difficulties themselves. But it is equally true that our fears often keep us from stepping out in faith, believing in ourselves, or even trusting in God.

This lesson will help teenagers discover the God who cares for them and will offer them God's promises during difficult days.

Before your students arrive, make sure to choose a wide range of pictures from the Internet that display or depict various fears: war, spiders, rejection, divorce, hunger, heights, poverty, disease, failure, or death. Begin the lesson by asking the students to each write down their top five fears on an index card. After a few minutes, show some of the photos on your laptop computer (or your projection system, if you're using a larger room at your church).

Then discuss:

- How has fear affected your life?

- How easily do you discuss your deepest fears with your friends?

- Do you ever feel ashamed about having fears? What impact does this have on you? How do you deal with that shame?

Read 1 John 4:13-19 aloud. Then ask:

- What do you think John meant when he wrote "perfect love expels all fear"?

- Do these verses mean Christians should never be afraid? Explain your answer.

- How can God's love comfort us during tough times?

- Some people say faith is the opposite of fear. Do you agree or disagree? Explain your perspective.

Close the lesson by asking students to divide into pairs and pray for each other. You also could sing a favorite praise song.

First Impressions

Big Idea: Encourage your teenagers to impersonate famous people

Age Level: middle school or high school

Maybe you have a few impersonations that you enjoy doing, and most likely, your students do, too. Invite them to share some of their impersonations. Mix it up by doing one of the following:

- Invite teenagers to impersonate a movie star or pop singer. See if the others in the group can guess the famous person.

- Invite teenagers to do their impersonations, and then have the group guess the identity by asking yes-or-no questions (such as "Are you living?" or "Are you a singer?").

- Invite the teenagers to re-enact a famous movie scene by taking on several roles. The rest of the students will try to guess the movie.

Fortune Cookie Thoughts

Big Idea: Search for real wisdom among the tasty treats

Supplies Needed: bag of fortune cookies

Age Level: middle school or high school

Purchase a $5 bag of fortune cookies. At your youth service, give each student a cookie. Say something like: "In a moment, I'll invite each of you to open your cookie and remove the fortune. Read the saying that is tucked inside your cookie, and think about it.

KEY

 Activity   **Games**   **Support**

(C) Camp/Retreats **(I)** Icebreaker **(T)** Teaching

(F) Food **(M)** Missions/Outreach **(W)** Worship

Does the saying make sense, does it hold true, and is it accurate for your life?"

Invite the teenagers to open their cookies together, and allow a minute or two for the students to consider their fortunes. Then ask:

- Who has a fortune that is true or wise? Why?

- Who has a fortune that you disagree with? Why?

- Ask the students to consider what they would write as a fortune.

- What Scripture passage would you include in the message?

- What relevant wisdom would you want to share with others through a fortune cookie message?

Close by praying that God would provide the teenagers with true wisdom and guidance.

Funny Glasses

Big Idea: Focus on staying serious while wearing silly eye gear

Supplies Needed: various funny glasses or masks, brown paper bag

Age Level: middle school or high school

For this game, collect several pairs of old eyeglasses, goggles, or Halloween eyewear. Place all these eyewear options in a brown paper bag. Gather your young people in a circle. Offer the bag to one teenager, who then begins the game. This teenager must reach into the bag, pick a pair of glasses, and put them on. Anyone who laughs is eliminated from the circle. Play continues around the circle until one person remains.

Make sure you have a few hilarious or outlandish pieces of eyewear. The more surprising or colorful, the better.

FANTASTIC FIVE for $5

WORSHIP IDEAS

There's nothing wrong with big-name bands, bright lights, and misty atmosphere to create a worship mood for teenagers. But when the budget gets tight, sometimes the music fades. Here are some ingenious ways to keep your youth worship vibrant even when the guitar strings break or you can't replace the drum heads.

1. Go Unplugged

If you live in an area where temperature and weather cooperate, take your worship service outdoors. You might save a little money, but you'll also create a great worship atmosphere.

Outdoor worship doesn't have to be fancy. You can do it on your own property, or travel a few miles down the road and find a suitable lawn area for a "stage." Some youth ministries have used shelter houses or gazebos at city or state parks to create a nice space for worship. Some may even go to camps, or find a suitable lawn area for staging and worship.

A few acoustic guitars, some drums or percussion instruments, maybe horns—that's all you need for a worshipful event. And if you go unplugged during the summer, you can create a camp environment with a makeshift fire pit, some lawn chairs, and a few candles.

2. iPod Experience

Most of your teenagers probably have iPods, so look for ways to incorporate these high-tech toys into your youth ministry. Create your own digital worship service in-house, or select some music that you think your teenagers would enjoy. For example, you could give your teenagers the name of a song or two for the upcoming week. They could download the digital files or access them from their own computers,

KEY

(A) Activity   (G) Games   (S) Support

(C) Camp/Retreats   (I) Icebreaker   (T) Teaching

(F) Food   (M) Missions/Outreach   (W) Worship

listen to the songs during the week, and then come to youth meeting the following week for a discussion of the lyrics and the message. Invite the teenagers to talk about how they felt or how the song affected their relationship with God.

Take along an iPod or other MP3 player when you're on the road for a mission project or some other trip.

Or if you have a small youth ministry or lead a small group, you could purchase five basic color iPod skins for $5 at a dollar store. Give one to each teenager, and invite the teenagers to use markers to decorate their iPod covers with a symbol that reflects their faith. Use these covers to lead the youth into a time of prayer as they discuss what their artwork means.

3. Listen to the Lyrics

Dig up lyrics to songs via the Internet, and read them aloud. Websites like christianlyricsonline.com and christian-lyrics.net are helpful resources. You can also find lyrics in the liner notes inside the CD case. Discuss the lyrics of favorite songs in this low-budget but unique worship service experience.

4. Go Gregorian

Maybe this won't work for everyone—but even the most sophisticated and high-tech youth ministry might get a bang out of going off the cuff with some Gregorian chanting of the psalms. It's not tough, especially if you can bring in a few example tracks to play. Invite the teenagers to join in. Open the Bible. Chant a psalm or two. Discuss the psalms and their place in worship through the centuries. Incorporate the Bible into worship and create your own chants (maybe even a signature chant).

5. Come Together, Yeah!

Has your youth worship experience been downsized, downplayed, overplayed, underplayed, or turned predictable and trite? Take your group on the road. Find another youth group willing to host a joint worship service—or several youth groups that would like to participate in one big service. Bring together your bands, musicians, and voices, and create a worship experience that will rock the place and bring your teenagers closer to God—and to other Christians in your community. Get together with other youth ministries and discover the power of praise.

Game Face Ⓖ Ⓒ

Big Idea: Paint faces to add spice to any game

Supplies Needed: bandages, lipstick, greasepaint, other types of makeup, paper towels, soap

Age Level: high school

To add a little spice, laughter, and downright hilarity to any game, invite each team to get ready for the competition by putting on their "game face." Provide bandages, lipstick, greasepaint, and other types of facial makeup for the teenagers to use. Encourage everyone to create a unified team face or faces that will intimidate the other players—or cause the other team to double over with laughter.

This added touch works really well with soccer, flag football, basketball, softball, or any large competitive game. It's a fun addition to church camp or retreat. Just be sure you have plenty of paper towels and soap for cleanup later.

KEY

Ⓐ Activity   Ⓖ Games   Ⓢ Support

Ⓒ Camp/Retreats   Ⓘ Icebreaker   Ⓣ Teaching

Ⓕ Food   Ⓜ Missions/Outreach   Ⓦ Worship

Give Worship Away (W)

Big Idea: Serve your church's seniors and shut-ins

Supplies Needed: guitar or other musical instrument, adult mentor, transportation

Age level: middle school or high school

Nearly every congregation has older members who are not able to leave their homes. Others may be confined to a health facility or rehab bed. Lift someone up by giving away your worship. Take your youth worship service to people who need the gentle touch of Christ and the witness of your teenagers. The students will provide a much-needed ministry, and they will also experience true worship as they give themselves in service and devotion to others.

Here's how you can do this. Organize a list of congregational members who are homebound or bedridden. Form worship teams (an acoustic guitar is the best instrument for this), and divide up your teenagers for visitation. Assign an adult mentor or chaperone for each group. Then make your visits.

Make each visit a mini-worship service, and ask the teenagers to take a leadership role as needed. Your worship will have a special meaning when you're ministering to people who especially need a warm embrace or a touch of God's love. And your older members will truly appreciate the teenagers.

A visitation worship service might look like this:

- Welcome and Introductions

- Opening Prayer

- Song or Hymn (sung by the group or by all)

- Psalm Reading

- Prayer (taking prayer requests and praying for one another)

- Song
- Bible Lesson
- Short Message or Testimony (from one of the teenagers)
- Song
- Closing Prayer

Go Online for Free Fun

Big Idea: Discover game ideas on the Internet

Supplies Needed: computer with Internet access

Age Level: middle school or high school

Check out these websites to get you started on ideas for indoor games, outdoor games, or just plain fun games.

youthministry.com features a variety of free resources produced by other youth workers. Check under the "Freebies" menu for some great ideas.

simplyyouthministry.com includes a section for "freebies" produced by the team at Simply Youth Ministry and their friends.

thesource4ym.com is a treasure trove of ideas. In particular, check out the "free resources and ideas" area. It's chocked-full of fun.

funattic.com is an all-purpose site devoted to providing hundreds of low-cost or no-cost game ideas. The area devoted to water games is one of the best for summer activities.

KEY

Ⓐ Activity	Ⓖ Games	Ⓢ Support
Ⓒ Camp/Retreats	Ⓘ Icebreaker	Ⓣ Teaching
Ⓕ Food	Ⓜ Missions/Outreach	Ⓦ Worship

brainbashers.com is a fine source for puzzles, brain teasers, and optical illusions. There are even card tricks here that you can play against the computer and logic puzzles that you can print out for a group. This stuff is perfect for a small group of brainiacs who enjoy expanding their minds.

seriouspuzzles.com is something akin to a novelty store for puzzles. Most of these puzzles listed here can be purchased for under $10, so if you are traveling in a bus or need a few low-budget games to occupy some time, this is a decent place to visit.

brainden.com has an incredible amount of riddles, puzzles, and optical illusions that are free. Much of the material on this site is also printable, which means you can take it with you on a retreat or can find it in a pinch.

Go Virtual

Big Idea: Travel the world without ever leaving town

Supplies Needed: computer with Internet access

Age Level: middle school or high school

We can go virtually anywhere in the world thanks to the Internet—or at least we can visit them virtually! Don't overlook the possibilities of having some virtual experiences as a group. Sound crazy? Maybe. But it can also be fun, educational, and exciting. Try taking one or more of these virtual tours—especially if your activities budget is virtually empty.

The Virtual World Tour
Do your homework by asking your teenagers to name their dream destinations; then find a few high-color websites that offer panoramic views of places your teenagers identified. Drop some of these photos into a presentation, or scroll through the sites on the big screen to experience the world in your youth room. You'll be in your hometown with the chips and dip, but your eyes and hearts can be in Hawaii, England, or virtually anywhere your mouse can take you.

The Virtual Mission Tour

If you can't take your group on a mission trip, bring the mission trip to your group. Ask the teenagers where they would like to be involved in a mission project. Then go online to find photos, information, and articles about the current mission efforts and the needs in that part of the world. Take time to pray for the mission efforts in that city, state, or nation—even as you visit online.

The Virtual Church

Take your teenagers on a virtual tour of other congregations' websites. Many of these sites feature videos you can watch, lectures or sermons you can listen to, articles you can read, devotions you can share, or photographs of events that can spark some of your own ideas. Visiting churches virtually is a fantastic way to gain new insights, see how others are sharing Christ's love, and even worship alongside people in another community or another part of the world.

The Virtual Laugh-In

Plenty of websites deliver lots of laughs: joke sites, church humor, cartoons, and more. Obviously, you can run into some rough stuff, too, but if you take control and exercise discretion in your search, you can find some hilarious content for your teenagers to enjoy—good clean fun, as they say. Set up a virtual laugh-in. Don't forget YouTube and Facebook as possible sources of laughter.

The Virtual Classroom

If your teenagers think they attend a boring school or lead a boring life, search online until you find some photos of the worst classrooms and schools imaginable. Seeing what other teenagers endure might just help your own teenagers count their blessings.

KEY

 Activity

 Games

 Support

 Camp/Retreats   **Icebreaker**   **Teaching**

 Food   **Missions/Outreach** **Worship**

The Virtual Oddity

If you are feeling truly adventurous, hold a contest to see which student can discover the weirdest, craziest website. You will need to review the sites before you show them to the rest of the group, of course, but we all know there are some clean-but-odd websites out there. Use the sites that deliver knockdown zaniness.

Goal Line Gospel

Big Idea: Take the field with a worship experience for guys

Supplies Needed: Bible, football, football helmet, shoulder pads, football cleats, music

Key Scriptures: Ephesians 6:13-18; Philippians 3:12-14

Age Level: middle school or high school

This worship experience is most suitable for the guys in your youth ministry—especially those who enjoy football or who might need some "coaching" in their faith. It will inspire, motivate, and challenge the guys to step up in their faith and discipleship.

The outline below shows key elements of the worship experience. Feel free to adapt it to fit your worship style, situation, or traditions.

Pre-Game Warm-up

Invite your teenagers to worship God with some upbeat music that will get their energy flowing and their minds prepared. Before or after these songs, say something like: "Every team must be prepared to step onto the field of play. And the same is true in life. We must be prepared to live out our faith, to stand strong in our convictions, and to live out what we profess. God is preparing us for great things. So let's get ready!"

Game Time

Read aloud Ephesians 6:13-18. Say something like: "As followers of Jesus, we need to make ourselves strong and suitable for work in God's kingdom. Just as a football player would never dream of stepping onto the field without a helmet, pads, and proper shoes, we need to put on the whole armor of God. We will need prayer, faith, courage, love, and conviction to carry us forward. We can only reach the goal by working together, by persevering in the face of adversity, and by doing what God has asked us to do. Christ is cheering us on, asking us to follow. And it is important that we not turn back in our faith."

Halftime

Sing more inspirational songs. Invite the teenagers to offer prayers for one another, for their families, and for their goals. As a leader, you could also give a "halftime" talk here, and reflect further on the Ephesians passage and what it means to you.

For a creative variation, tape your halftime message ahead of time. Play your message as a pep talk for the group. And be sure to use your football equipment and incorporate all of it into your message. Have fun with this worship experience. It will be an uplifting time for your guys.

You Have to Sacrifice

Discuss the significance of stewardship and why we should offer our lives to God. You could also receive an offering of money or ask students to make other commitments at this time. Say something like: "No team can reach the goal without sacrifice. The same is true of the church. If we are a part of God's team, we must be willing to sacrifice if God is going to help us be victorious. The coach can't play the game for us. We have to be willing to participate in the work and demonstrate our faith every day. That is why we give. It is why we sacrifice our time, talent, and treasure."

Second Half

Read aloud Philippians 3:12-14. Say something like: "We have a goal and purpose for our lives. Our purpose is to glorify God in all that we say

KEY

 Activity

 Camp/Retreats

 Food

 Games

 Icebreaker

 **Missions/Outreach**

 Support

Teaching

Worship

and do, to help others find a path to Christ, and to proclaim the good news of Jesus and his love. But achieving this goal is not easy. We need to persevere. Sometimes we face adversity. Sometimes we struggle. Sometimes we give up. Sometimes we don't properly prepare to achieve what God desires for our lives. But we must press on toward the victory, which God has already won for us in Christ."

Post-Game Analysis

Invite some of the teenagers to share their testimonies, or ask them to reflect on what they learned from Scripture.

- What have you learned from these Bible passages?

- What inspiration and guidance have you received from the Bible today?

Victory Celebration

Sing more inspiring songs. Return to Ephesians 6:13-18 for one more reading. Close your worship experience with a prayer, or ask the teenagers to shout together: "We are victorious in Christ!"

God Keeps Providing

Big Idea: Dig deep with a four-part series on stewardship

Supplies Needed: index cards, pencils, Bibles, whiteboard, markers

Lesson Length: 20 minutes per module

Key Scriptures: 2 Kings 4:1-7; 4:38-44; 5:1-2, 9-14; Psalm 23

Age Level: high school

Each of these four teaching modules will help your teenagers understand biblical stewardship. You might choose to use them over a one-month span at your weekly youth meetings, or you could incorporate them into a retreat. The focus of each module is teaching young people about God's blessings and provision during tough times.

Module 1: God Provides

Key Scripture: 2 Kings 4:1-7

Begin this lesson by asking the teenagers to complete the following sentences:

- When life gets tough, I usually respond by…

- When good things happen for me, I usually think about…

Following the responses and discussion, say something like: "Let's now check out a biblical account about the prophet Elisha. He lived during a time when the people of Israel experienced famine and drought, and life was incredibly difficult. Let's see how he dealt with a lean time."

Read the Scripture passage aloud and then ask:

- What surprises you most about how Elisha dealt with this difficult situation? Why?

- How did Elisha demonstrate his trust in God to provide for the need?

- What can you learn from this biblical account about our own challenges and how God can help us deal with them?

Now take a few minutes to discuss how God is our provider; then ask the teenagers to make a list on the whiteboard of some of the things that God has provided for them.

Ask:

- Which is a bigger miracle: God providing an answer in a huge, awesome way; or God providing an answer through small daily events? Explain your perspective.

- Do you think it is easier or more difficult to see God's provision during a tough time? Explain your answer.

Close by asking the teenagers to pray about areas of their lives where they need God's help.

KEY

(A) Activity   (G) Games   (S) Support

(C) Camp/Retreats   (i) Icebreaker   (T) Teaching

(F) Food   (M) Missions/Outreach   (W) Worship

Module 2: God Transforms

Key Scripture: 2 Kings 4:38-41

Open the lesson by distributing index cards and pencils. Ask the teenagers to make a list of three things they would change about the world. Then have one or two students read their lists.

Ask these questions:

- Why is it often difficult for dreams of transformation in our world to become realities?

- How would you describe God's role in transforming our world?

- Read 2 Kings 4:38-41 aloud, then ask:

    - What does this Bible account tell you about God's transforming power in a time of need?

    - How did God change things in this passage?

    - What connections do you see between our human needs and God's power to transform a dire situation?

Invite the teenagers to write on the backs of their index cards as they answer the following questions. Tell your students that no one will be asked to share his or her answers with the group:

- What is one thing you would like God to transform in your life?

- What is one thing you would like God to help you transform in your world?

Close the lesson with a time of silent reflection.

Module 3: God Blesses

Key Scripture: 2 Kings 4:42-44

Begin by asking the teenagers to complete the following sentence:

- My greatest blessing from God is…

Write some of their responses on the whiteboard.

Afterward, read 2 Kings 4:42-44 aloud and say something like: "Elisha was a great prophet who trusted God in all things. Elisha knew that God blessed, and he knew that God could take a little and make much from it. We may not see the possibilities that exist in our hands and in our blessings, but if we give our gifts to God, God can bless them and make them larger."

Ask the teenagers these questions:

- Why would God choose to bless people in this particular way? Explain your answer.

- Why would God provide "leftovers," instead of just providing the exact amount of food needed?

- What lessons do you see in this biblical account?

Ask the teenagers to find partners, and then distribute index cards and pencils. Challenge each pair to make a list of blessings your youth group needs (for example, more unity, more compassion, or more joy). After a few minutes, ask each pair to share what they wrote down. Discuss these blessings, and close by asking God to provide what you need.

Module 4: God Restores
Key Scripture: 2 Kings 5:1-2, 9-14; Psalm 23

Begin by reading aloud the biblical story. Afterward, discuss the story by asking:

- Why do you think Naaman wanted to be healed of his leprosy?

- Are you surprised by how upset Naaman becomes in verses 11 and 12? Explain your answer.

Then say something like: "Sometimes God directs us to do difficult tasks. But most of the time, God simply wants us to live faithfully right where we are and to focus on being faithful with the little things of life. We

KEY

 Activity

 Games

 Support

 Camp/Retreats

 Icebreaker

 Teaching

 Food

Missions/Outreach

Worship

don't have to do spectacular things for God to be faithful. In this story from 2 Kings, Naaman was angry with the prophet and with God because he thought his healing should have been difficult, not easy."

Then ask:

- What are some of the "little things" in your life right now that are helping you become more faithful in following God? How are they shaping your spiritual growth? Explain your answer.

- What was the last "big thing" God asked you to do? Did you obey God? Talk about that experience and what happened.

- Do you believe God can heal and restore someone who is sick, hurt, or depressed? Explain your answer.

Distribute index cards and pencils, and ask the teenagers to write down three things they would like to see God restore in their lives (for example, confidence, hope, family income). After a few minutes, close the lesson with a time of silence, or read aloud Psalm 23.

Goin' to the Chapel ⓣ

Big Idea: Examine true love and the marriage commitment

Key Scripture: 1 Corinthians 13

Supplies Needed: wedding ring as an object lesson, Bible, photocopies of the words to a wedding ceremony

Lesson Length: 45 minutes

Age Level: high school

Begin the lesson by holding up a wedding ring and asking:

- What comes to mind when you see a ring like this?

- What does a ring say that words cannot?

Distribute copies of the wedding ceremony, and then ask the students to study the words the bride and groom use as they give their vows and exchange their rings. Then ask:

- What is significant about the words that a bride and groom say to each other?

- With divorce so common in our culture, do the promises of a wedding ceremony hold meaning anymore? Explain your perspective.

- What is God's role in a marriage relationship?

Read aloud 1 Corinthians 13. Then ask:

- How would you define the kind of love that the Apostle Paul describes here?

- How is this type of love fulfilled in marriage?

- Do you think it is possible for a man or a woman to love their spouse more than themselves? Explain your answer.

- How or when do a husband and wife need to rely upon God in marriage?

- What excites you about marriage?

- What scares you about marriage?

Close the lesson by reading the wedding vows aloud and sharing some of your own insights about marriage. Invite your spouse, if willing, to also offer some comments and wisdom. If you're single, talk about how the idea of marriage excites you and scares you.

KEY

(A) Activity   (G) Games   (S) Support

(C) Camp/Retreats   (I) Icebreaker   (T) Teaching

(F) Food   (M) Missions/Outreach   (W) Worship

Going Deeper ⓣ ⓘ

Big Idea: Use simple things to launch deep conversations

Supplies Needed: cups, tools, envelopes, chairs
(depending on the lesson)

Lesson Length: 20 minutes

Age Level: middle school to high school

The following lessons can be used in youth meetings, in staff meetings, or in youth team meetings. Each lesson offers a unique and creative approach, and you can easily obtain the items needed for all the ideas. These lessons don't require much prep time, and they generate open-ended discussions. I've used these ideas for years, and each time, I discover something new about our teenagers, our team members, or myself. These are easy but effective lessons that will stir deep conversations and revelations. You will likely learn how people are feeling, what they are experiencing, and how they view themselves — including their hurts, pains, and joys. Simply put: These are concise yet powerful lessons.

Cups

Assemble an array of various-sized cups, and place water of varying amounts in the cups before your meeting begins. Make sure the collection of cups is diverse enough to provide options and thoughtful deliberation.

When the group gathers, invite everyone to examine the cups. Go around the group, and ask each person to openly and honestly answer this question:

- Which cup best represents you at this very moment, and why?

Tools

Bring in a tool chest or tool box filled with various items: screwdriver, hammer, tape measure, bolts, screws, wire, duct tape, clippers, ruler, chisel, electrical parts, tin snips, clamp, saw, square, and so on.

You get the picture—the more, the better.

Gather your group together. Invite everyone to examine all of the tools. Then ask each person to choose the tool that best answers the following question:

- Which tool best represents what you need from God right now, and why?

Ask each person to share with the group honestly and openly.

Colors

Go to a hardware store or paint store and obtain samples from a few dozen different paint colors and styles. Make sure you have a wide variety of hues. Place these strips on a table. Invite your group to examine the colors and then select a color that best answers the following question:

- Which color best represents what you are experiencing in your life right now, and why?

Encourage everyone to share openly and honestly.

Envelopes

Collect a bunch of various-sized envelopes for display. Place these on a table before your meeting. Invite everyone to examine the selection carefully and then choose an envelope that best answers the following question:

- Which envelope best represents the size and shape of your faith right now, and why?

Ask everyone to share openly and honestly with the group.

KEY

 Activity   Games   Support

 Camp/Retreats   Icebreaker   Teaching

 Food   Missions/Outreach   Worship

Screensavers

Before your meeting, select 10 to 20 screensaver images that you can display. Prepare these on a laptop, and as your group or team gathers, scroll through the set three times and ask everyone to select a screensaver image that best answers the following question:

- Which screensaver image best represents how you see your life right now, and why?

Discuss openly and honestly with the group.

Chairs

Before the meeting, select an array of various sized, shaped, and contoured chairs. (You'll have more chairs around a church than you might expect!) Try to find a good mix of chairs: metal folding chairs, padded seats, reclining desk chairs, and so on. If you can get a range of colors, that's an added bonus.

Invite each person to sit in or stand next to the chair that best answers this question:

- My greatest need is best represented by this chair because…

Encourage openness and honesty among the group.

Movies

Bring in a cornucopia of movie DVDs. Display them on a table. Invite everyone to consider the movies on display, and ask each person to select one that best answers this question:

- A movie plot that reminds me of my life is… because…

Have fun with these and be prepared to learn a lot about your teenagers or the people in your leadership group!

MISSION/OUTREACH IDEAS

Outreach and mission efforts—especially to, for, and with our teenagers—are vital to our faithfulness as God's people. Even during tough times, we can't compromise our desire to reach other teenagers with the message of God's love. Here are five ways to do more outreach and evangelism with less money in your youth account.

1. Tell the Story

Teenagers appreciate honesty. And if they know the score, they'll do more! If your outreach and evangelism budget is taking a hit, be open and honest with your teenagers. Don't cast the truth in a negative light, but give your students the opportunity to step up to the plate and make a difference. Get the young people involved in new forms of outreach and mission efforts. Your teenagers will likely have some new ideas of their own.

2. Stay Local

Many youth ministries have a traditional summer mission trip. But when funds get tight, these trips may be more difficult to finance. Consider staying local for your mission effort. You'll either eliminate or significantly reduce your expenses, and you'll discover incredible ministry opportunities among your neighbors. Don't fall into the trap of thinking that you have to travel great distances to find a need or to minister to a hurting community.

Here's a variation: If you have resources for a mission trip, still keep your team local, but send finances to churches or ministries that are serving people in another state or country. Maybe you'll be helping victims of a hurricane, tornado, or flood. Maybe you'll be providing food for an inner-city soup kitchen. Maybe you'll be financing mosquito nets to stop the spread of malaria. By partnering with other churches or ministries, you are able to give them more by traveling less!

3. Try Texting Evangelism

Get out the word for your next big event, outreach effort, or social event with text messages. It's an idea that can help you reach disconnected or unchurched teenagers. Prepare a basic template description of your event (160 characters or less), and invite your teenagers to send the word out to friends via a text message on their cell phones. It's a fast and effective way for your youth group to get news and events to dozens of other teenagers.

4. Coupon Outreach

Some years back, our youth group partnered with a fast-food restaurant to create our own coupon. We got permission from the restaurant owners to create a coupon with a special offer, and the back featured information about our church and youth ministry.

Of course, it helped that the restaurant owner was also a member of the church! But I've always been pleasantly surprised at what restaurants and businesses are willing to do to help a vibrant youth group.

Once you have the coupons produced, your students can distribute them to friends and neighbors, or place them in high-traffic areas around town. A coupon is a win-win. The people who use them get a nice deal, and they also get an invitation to visit your youth group or congregation.

5. Food Pantry Party

If you have a food pantry that is serving the needs of your community, try a one-day mission and see how much food you can gather in a single afternoon. First, get the support of the local pantry organizers, and ask them to endorse your efforts. Then do the mission project. Here's how:

Divide the teenagers into teams of two to four (with at least one adult or chaperone per group). Give each group the name and location of several grocery stores, shopping centers, convenience stores, or restaurants. Make sure you have addresses and a road map for each group. Contacts at each location would also be helpful.

Disperse into the community, visit each store, and ask the managers if they would be willing to donate canned food or boxed items (these usually transport best) to the local food pantry. Many will be glad to donate at least a small amount of food to the cause, and with everyone working together it is surprising how much food you can gather in a single afternoon. Transport this to your pantry, and gather back at the home base to celebrate how you've helped a worthy cause.

Going to the Dogs

Big Idea: Get creative with dog food

Supplies Needed: dry dog food, paper towels

Age Level: middle school

This activity is a real "howler." Purchase $5 worth of dry dog food or assorted dog biscuits. Make sure you buy dog food that is composed of various colors, not just one variety. (Hint: Buy from a dollar store.)

Divide the youth into teams of two or three, and give each team a paper towel and several handfuls of the dry dog food. Challenge the teams to use the dog food to create the most unusual image of a canine on their paper towel. The dog food will stay in place on the towel, and the teams can use the various colors and hues to create visual images, shapes, and outlines.

The team that creates the best dog image on the paper towel gets to divide the dog food and take it home to their pets.

KEY

(A) Activity	(G) Games	(S) Support
(C) Camp/Retreats	(I) Icebreaker	(T) Teaching
(F) Food	(M) Missions/Outreach	(W) Worship

Graduation Worship Experience ⓦ

Big Idea: Creatively honor your high school graduates

Supplies Needed: simple worship and celebration supplies such as music, Bible readings, easy refreshments, address book

Age Level: high school

Enlist the help of your high school freshmen, sophomores, and juniors to plan this special worship service to honor your high school graduates. Your graduation worship experience doesn't have to be elaborate; in fact, simplicity enhances the event. Offer some good music, some meaningful Scripture and prayer, and some opportunities for reflection. Let your seniors shine. Give every senior a chance to step to the microphone and speak briefly about future plans and dreams.

These worship experiences can also honor graduates' parents—make sure you invite them to attend. Consider having a reception afterward; punchbowl and refreshments can't be beat.

A final word: Make sure you get the new addresses of your graduating seniors (their college, military, or home addresses), and do your best to stay in touch with them.

Great Adventures (A) (T)

Big Idea: Find alternative destinations for fun activities

Supplies Needed: light lunches, Bibles, challenge-course materials and tools, transportation, adult chaperones (depending on the specific activity)

Age Level: middle school or high school

Maybe you've had to reduce the number of trips and activities for your youth ministry because of limited finances. You may no longer have a large enough budget to subsidize youth trips to amusement parks, ski resorts, or summer camps. Perhaps this is the best time to create new activities or rediscover some of the simple, classic outings that teenagers have enjoyed for years. The "big event" may become a small event, but it can still entertain your teenagers and help them develop stronger friendships.

Here are some classic low-budget or no-budget activities that can pump some life into your youth ministry. With limited mileage, you should be able to do any of these on $5 or less.

Gather at the River

You probably have a river or large stream within reasonable driving distance. Historically, metaphorically, and theologically, a river offers some fantastic opportunities for teaching, socializing, and relaxing. That trip to the river could turn into a spiritually meaningful experience for your teenagers.

Pack a lunch, or ask your students to bring their own lunches from home. Find a nice, quiet area for a picnic and time of conversation. Bring a Bible. Discuss some of the river metaphors and theological implications of water. (How about the Jordan River in Joshua 3? David's imagery in

KEY

(A) **Activity**   (G) **Games**   (S) **Support**

(C) **Camp/Retreats**   (I) **Icebreaker**   (T) **Teaching**

(F) **Food**   (M) **Missions/Outreach** (W) **Worship**

Psalm 23? The vision at the Kebar River in Ezekiel 1? The baptism of Jesus in Mark 1?)

A riverside seat is a perfect setting for a youth outing. You don't have to drive far, and with a bit of planning, you'll create a fantastic opportunity to teach and challenge your group.

Stress-Challenge Course

For this particular activity, I highly recommend you check with your senior pastor or elder board, since it requires the use of church property. I would also encourage you to obtain the permission of parents for their teenager(s) to participate in this challenge.

You can find varieties and levels of these types of courses: ropes courses, high wires fitted with safety ropes and chains, rope bridges, walking planks. There is likely an adventure course near you; church camps, YMCA camps, and scout camps are great places to begin a search if your group wants to go this direction.

The courses may cost little, though some of the more challenging ones often involve a small fee to hire a professional course instructor to guide your group through the adventure.

And don't overlook the possibility of creating your own challenge course. If your church property includes an area of trees, trails, or some semblance of an "outback," you can probably create a moderately challenging course on your own (you might need a bit of engineering help from skilled people in your congregation). Challenge courses can be designed on a dime using scrap wood, rope, and perhaps some cable. Visit some of the challenge courses nearby or search for pictures of courses online to get ideas. Then implement your concept in a low-impact, safe design that fits your group and level of experience.

The Lakeshore

Much like the river destination, consider all of the fellowship and teaching opportunities that can accompany a visit to a lake. No doubt there are several options in your area. Over the years I've taken groups to small, private lakes where we met in cabins or on property owned by church members. We've also traveled to much larger lakes where we hiked and camped and discussed the lake stories in the Gospels (for example, the disciples' experiences on the Sea of Galilee). A lakeside adventure is a low-cost option that can yield high-octane outcomes.

The Cemetery

At first glance, this destination may seem a rather morbid or misdirected place for a youth gathering. But you can create some exhilarating, honest, and open discussions with teenagers on cemetery grounds. In fact, it's often older adults who have difficulty with walking through a cemetery, meeting at the graves of beloved friends, or taking flowers to graves on Memorial Day.

Teenagers, on the other hand, always seem willing to talk about the big themes of life and death, our hope of eternal life, the faith we place in the resurrection of Jesus, and what his life means to us. When done with the proper attitude, there's no disrespect in meeting in a cemetery. In fact, meeting among the memorials to the dead can be extremely powerful.

Here are a few ideas. Visit a cemetery on Good Friday. Discuss the meaning and significance of Jesus' death and resurrection. Visit the grave of a friend or family member. Memorialize this person, and discuss how our faith intersects with the realities of death and our unwillingness to face death. Visit a cemetery to talk about life! Why is it important for me to enjoy life now? What do I need to say? What do I need to do? What is the purpose of my life? If you haven't had these discussions in a cemetery, you are missing a powerful opportunity to engage teenagers in real, deep, genuine talk!

The Orchard

If you are looking for a wonderful fall destination for your group, consider a trip to a local orchard. Orchards offer a fantastic sensory experience, and for a few dollars you can enjoy a wonderfully delicious time and a peaceful setting for learning or conversation. This adventure is so low-key, it's just fun. And as for learning opportunities, they are ripe for the plucking.

KEY

 Activity

 Camp/Retreats

Food

 Games

Icebreaker

 Missions/Outreach

 Support

 Teaching

 Worship

Don't overlook the orchard if your activities budget is running
on empty.

The Lighthouse

If you live near a coastline, take your teenagers to a lighthouse. Talk
about being a light for God, or discuss God's guidance and protection
through the dangerous rocks and waves of life. No doubt you can have
some meaningful discussions about faith during your lighthouse visit.

The Christmas Tree Farm

This concept is similar to the orchard visit, but this variation takes your
group to a fun-filled pre-Christmas destination. Many Christmas tree
farms serve up delicious opportunities for youth groups such as snacks,
hot chocolate, campfires, and candied apples. A Christmas tree farm is a
wonderful setting for a lesson on the birth of Jesus. A starry night makes
the visit all the more mystical. And, yes, this one will cost very little. It's
great for the budget and the soul.

Greet Them With a Card

Big Idea: Unleash teenage creativity on greeting cards

Supplies Needed: paper, markers, stickers, computer, printer

Age Level: middle school or high school

If your teenagers are creative and energetic, and if they enjoy drawing,
writing, and cutting, try making greeting cards. People will eagerly buy
cards that have a personal touch and also support your teenagers.
Concentrate on birthday cards and get-well wishes. Depending on the
season, you could also create cards for Valentine's Day, Mother's Day,
Father's Day, Thanksgiving, or Christmas.

You can also create simple sets of cards on card stock and print these on
a computer printer. If you go this route, make thank-you cards, thinking-of-
you cards, and blank cards. These should sell well.

If you can set up a display for these cards in a high-traffic area at church, you'll likely sell everything you create.

High School Exam

Big Idea: Help students consider their next steps after high school

Supplies Needed: photocopies of **"The Exam" handout (p. 173)**

Lesson Length: 30 minutes

Age Level: seniors in high school

This lesson will help your high school seniors reflect upon the highlights of their high school years and also help them prepare for the next steps. Give each student a copy of the exam, and follow up by asking students to divide into pairs to discuss a few of their answers. If you have enough time or a small enough group, bring together all of the seniors for a few minutes of conversation at the end of your lesson.

KEY

 Activity    Games   Support

 Camp/Retreats   Icebreaker   Teaching

Food   Missions/Outreach   Worship

Honey, Do You Love Me? Ⓖ Ⓒ Ⓘ

Big Idea: Make your friends laugh with silly words and faces

Supplies Needed: none

Age Level: middle school or high school

In this funny icebreaker game, everyone sits on chairs in a circle. One teenager begins by choosing another person in the group, walking up to that student, and asking, "Honey, do you love me?" This person must then respond: "Honey, I love you, but I just can't smile." If either person laughs, they are eliminated from the game. If neither person laughs, the responder becomes the questioner and walks up to another person. Play continues until the last person is eliminated via laughter.

The object, of course, is to avoid laughing—but it's also a good strategy to ask the question or give the response in a voice or with a facial expression that will eliminate the other person. Using crossed eyes, picking the nose, or using a high falsetto voice are sure winners to eliminate a few people in short order.

Human Checkers Ⓖ

Big Idea: Turn teenagers into game pieces in your parking lot

Supplies Needed: Chalk line, chalk, duct tape

Age Level: middle school or high school

If your church has a large asphalt parking lot, create a large checkerboard with some sidewalk chalk.

Once you've drawn the board, invite your teenagers to be the human checkers. They can wear hats or specific shirts to designate the two colors of checkers.

Smaller groups of teenagers may play each other, or two people can play by "moving" the human pieces around the board.

Naturally, you will need sufficient numbers of teenagers to play human checkers, but it is great fun. And for variety, you could also try playing Tick-Tack-Toe or Chess.

Here are two variations on creating the checkerboard. One, use a chalk line and duct tape to create a slick-looking checkerboard. Two, if you don't have an adequate parking lot (or permission to draw on it), use ropes to create a checkerboard in the grass.

I Hear Voices

Big Idea: Collect voice mail messages to inspire teenagers on trips

Supplies Needed: small tape recorder

Age Level: high school

Use this activity to encourage your teenagers during a mission trip or a retreat. A few weeks ahead of your departure date, invite your students' parents to leave a voice mail message for their son or daughter on your telephone. Collect these encouraging voice mails, record them onto a small, handheld recorder, and then take them on your trip.

Play these encouraging messages to the group after you've arrived at your mission destination or your retreat. This activity is touching, rousing, and helpful as a means of encouraging your teenagers and bringing the group together.

KEY

 Activity   **Games**   **Support**

 Camp/Retreats   **Icebreaker**    **Teaching**

 Food   **Missions/Outreach**   **Worship**

I Remember (A)

Big Idea: Introduce teenagers to people they've never met

Supplies Needed: none

Age Level: middle school or high school

This game works well when you are doing introductions or when you have two groups of teenagers that need to get acquainted. Instruct the teenagers to find partners—but they must find someone they haven't met before. Allow five to 10 minutes for the teenagers to talk to each other.

Ask the pairs to discuss these questions if they need to keep conversation flowing:

- What drives you nuts?
- What is one food you won't eat?
- What is your worst habit?
- What's your favorite slang expression?

Once the teenagers have completed this activity, ask each person to repeat back three things they remember about the other person. Or use this exercise to help one teenager introduce the other person to the group.

Identity Theft

Big Idea: Consider faith as an identifying feature of our lives

Key Bible Verses: Matthew 16:24-26; 18:1-5

Supplies Needed: whiteboard, markers, paper, pencils, Bibles

Lesson Length: 40 minutes

Age Level: high school

Begin the lesson by asking your teenagers to define identity theft. Write their suggested definitions on the whiteboard. Then ask these questions:

- What are some differences between stealing a person's identity and impersonating someone?

- What aspects of your identity would be the most frightening to lose? Why?

- Have you known anyone who was a victim of identity theft? How did that person cope with this? What did it take to regain his or her identity?

Distribute paper and pencils along with the Bibles. Divide the teenagers into pairs. Give each group one of the following Bible passages to study:

- Matthew 16:24-26

- Matthew 18:1-5

In groups, ask the students to discuss and write down their observations and answers to the following questions about the assigned biblical passages:

- How would you describe the new identity Jesus is discussing in this passage?

- Would it be easy or difficult to assume this new identity? Explain your perspective.

- What are some of the key characteristics of the new identity Jesus is asking us to assume?

Bring your students back together, and ask each pair to offer up one or two insights about the identifying characteristics of being a follower of Jesus. Write some of these on the whiteboard.

Close the session by reading 2 Corinthians 5:16-17 aloud and praying silently as your teenagers consider what it means to be a new person in Christ.

Interactive Webcast Worship Experience

Big Idea: Connect with Christians in another nation

Supplies Needed: webcast capability

Age Level: middle school or high school

Years ago, ham radio operators used to see if they could make contact with operators in other countries, and now we can do the same thing via computer. Furthermore, we can worship together with people living on the other side of the world.

If you have the capability to do a webcast, work with your church leaders to create an interactive worship experience with a missionary or congregation in another country. With the advent of Skype™ technology, we can now have simulcast experiences directly from our computers and webcams. With some organizational work, you should be able to broadcast a worship service to another computer in another nation—or, at the very least, several states away.

Internet Radio Station (W)

Big Idea: Use digital technology for a radio broadcast

Supplies Needed: computer with Internet access, microphones, recording equipment

Age Level: high school

This isn't science fiction. In fact, the day of the Internet radio station is upon us. In the not too distant future, all radio stations may be broadcast via the Internet, and stations with towers and dedicated frequencies may become a technology of the past.

But you don't have to wait until then; you can have your own online radio station today and broadcast a worship service, music, youth announcements, or other programming. Here's how.

Check out live365.com for a listing of the hundreds of online radio stations that already exist. In particular, listen to some of the stations listed under the "inspirational" category. You'll find a few churches, along with some stations devoted to sacred music.

This site also contains information that can help you design your own radio station. Depending on your congregation's technical skills, you may not have to invest a single dime in new equipment to get started.

For example, if you are already broadcasting adult worship services, youth services, or music via streaming audio on your ministry's website, you can likely set up a bare-bones station with minimal work and no investment. Likewise, you may already be recording your own worship talks on CD, and this can be a source of digital information that you can use on your radio station.

KEY

 (A) Activity

 (G) Games

 (S) Support

(C) Camp/Retreats

(I) Icebreaker

 (T) Teaching

 (F) Food

 (M) Missions/Outreach

 (W) Worship

Inviting an Expert

Big Idea: Identify someone with a message teenagers need to hear

Supplies Needed: none

Age Level: high school

This simple idea can yield huge dividends for your teenagers. Ask everyone to sit in a circle and tackle the following three questions:

- What is one subject you would like to learn about?

- What questions would you ask about this topic if we had an expert here right now?

- What expert can we invite to speak to us? Or where could we find an expert?

In just a few minutes, your group could come up with a short list of people whom they would invite to speak on the chosen subject matter—or at least some ideas where you might be able to find this person. Invite your expert to speak to your group on the chosen topic, and encourage all of your teenagers to attend.

It's a Teen Thing

Big Idea: Honor your Creator during your teenage years

Key Bible Verses: Ecclesiastes 12:1-7

Supplies Needed: Bible

Lesson Length: 10 minutes

Age Level: middle school or high school

To begin the lesson, ask the students to form a circle, and invite each one to complete the phrase: "It's a teen thing when…" (Nothing profane, of course.) For example, "It's a teen thing when you go to Friday night football games" or "It's a teen thing when you send 300 text messages a day."

Watch for patterns to emerge, and see if there are ideas or concepts that the teenagers in your group consider uniquely "young."

Next, read aloud Ecclesiastes 12:1-7. (Check out Eugene Peterson's *The Message* for a great rendition here!)

Then ask:

- Do you think teen things are only enjoyed by young people? Explain your answer.

- What's the main idea you see in this passage of Ecclesiastes? What's the author trying to tell you?

- How can you continue learning as you grow older? Give us some examples.

Close by reading Ecclesiastes 12:1-2 again.

KEY

 Activity

 Camp/Retreats

Food

Games

Icebreaker

Missions/Outreach

 Support

 Teaching

Worship

Just People ⓖ ⓒ ⓘ

Big Idea: Play games that only require humans

Supplies Needed: none

Age Level: middle school or high school

Many fantastic games require no supplies at all—just people. If you have an open space and plenty of energy, try one or two of these games. The youth group itself is all you need for some great fun.

Group-Up

This simple game involves quick movement and anticipation. The youth leader will simply clap a certain number of times. The teenagers must then get into groups of that number. So if you clap three times, everyone must be in a group of three. As you play this game, some people will be "leftovers"—you may have one or two students left if you clapped three times. These people are then eliminated from the game. Continue to play until only two people remain.

People-to-People

This game can be played with large groups. Invite one person to serve as the first leader of this game, and everyone else should find a partner. The leader gives "body" instructions that the pairs must follow. For example: "Elbow to Elbow" means that each group will place their elbows together. "Finger to Knee" means one person must place a finger on the partner's knee. (Be sure to institute and follow a "nothing obscene" rule.)

The leader instructs the pairs through a few body movements, and then yells, "People-to-People!" Each person must immediately find a new partner, including the leader. The odd person out becomes the new leader, and play continues for as long as you like.

Circle In, Circle Out

This simple game involves balance and coordination. Invite everyone to form a circle by holding hands. Count around the circle by Ones and Twos. A leader then instructs the Ones to lean in while the Twos lean out. The group will need to work together to balance the circle. Then the leader reverses the instruction, with the Twos leaning in and the Ones leaning out.

Continue play until the group begins to feel the balance and coordination necessary to make this transition. Then see how quickly the group can change positions with the instruction. It's fun to watch.

Can You Do This?

Form a circle. Invite one teenager to enter the circle and lead the group. The leader says, "Can you do this?" and does a funny, awkward, limber, or contorted movement. The other teenagers in the circle then try to do this same movement in exactly the same way. This is a good warm-up game and usually involves a lot of stretching.

The Lineup

This fun game can help your teenagers build new friendships. Place 10 to 15 people in a row (like a lineup at a police station). One person will stand in front of the lineup, and each person will introduce himself or herself to the individual. The individual will then turn around, and one person in the lineup will move to a new place. When the individual turns around to face the lineup again, he or she must identify which person has changed spots.

High Fives

Use this game as an icebreaker. Have your students form a line. One person will walk down the line giving a high five to everyone along the way. Each person must then say his/her first name when receiving a high five. This is a fast way to share names and greet each other. Everyone should go down the line once, and by the end of the game, teenagers will have met some new friends.

KEY

 Activity

 Camp/Retreats

 Food

 Games

 Icebreaker

 Missions/Outreach

 Support

Teaching

Worship

My Famous Friend

Consider playing this game when you're doing introductions at a retreat or camp. Invite the teenagers to find partners. After some introduction time for each pair, invite the teenagers to introduce their partners as famous people. The famous person's appearance or personality could resemble the teenager's. This is a fun group-builder that will launch your outing with a friendly start.

FANTASTIC FIVE for $5

FOOD IDEAS

When it comes to food and fun, you'll find one or more of these ideas to be just the tasty treat you're looking for.

1. Sack-Lunch Outing

If your activity funds are running low, but you still have enough gas in the tank to take your teenagers on a day trip, do a brown-bag lunch outing. It's a simple solution to a complex problem. Invite each teenager to pack a lunch in a brown paper bag (sandwich, chips, cookies, fruit, and any food that won't spoil in the heat). Bring the meals on your outing to a state park, a scenic overlook, a day trip to the mall, or any place that doesn't have admission costs or other charges. It's great fun for the cost of a tank of gas.

You can also spice up your brown-bag excursion a bit by having a competition. Give small prizes to the best-decorated bag, the cleanest bag at the end of the day (or the one with the fewest grease stains), the most pristine bag, the best packed lunch, and so on.

2. Healthy Options

We're all becoming more aware of the unhealthy eating habits of the average American. This is especially true for teenagers, who rely upon a steady diet of fast-food and junk food. But the church doesn't have to buy into the habit. Instead, our youth ministries can be a source of healthy testimony when it comes to food.

Instead of doughnuts, serve yogurt, fruit, and juices. Or how about a lunch of whole wheat sandwiches, carrot sticks, and milk instead of chicken nuggets, potato chips, and cookies? And for your next overnight event, try serving up a healthy batch of vegetable lasagna or vegetable stew instead of hamburgers, hot dogs, and brownies.

And here's a bonus—these healthy options can actually be less expensive than the fast-food options. Many can be prepared for $5. So when times get tough, get healthy. Your dollars will go further, and you and your students will feel better, too.

3. Go Green

Use the "green" machine to save money. For example, many congregations are opting out of paper plates, plastic bowls and cups, and other disposable kitchenware, and choosing to use plates, cups, and saucers that can be washed and reused. Many youth groups have found a valuable role washing the dishes after dinners (with a bit of fun added) and are getting some additional exercise to boot. Plus, many teenagers have never had the experience of washing dishes, so don't deprive them of this hands-on learning!

4. Trail Mix

Try this snack option to produce lots of food on a $5 budget. Make your own trail mix. There are a lot of recipes, but you can't go wrong with a simple combination of peanuts, raisins, and bits of chocolate. Visit a dollar store and see how much you can actually mix for $5. And if you can budget $5 a week to make this snack, you can save any left-over trail mix in an airtight container, adding new trail mix each week.

This is a low-cost option for weekly youth group snacks or for food that you can take on your trips and retreats.

5. Summer Garden

If you have lots of green space on your church grounds, use some of it to start a garden and grow your own food. With a $5 supply of seeds and some willing volunteers, you can produce some vegetable snacks that your students would enjoy. Try this:

- Partition off a 10x10-foot space for the garden, and plant carrots, celery, and tomatoes. These are basic vegetable snacks that can be enjoyed later in the summer.

- Weed and till the garden weekly.

- Invite the teenagers to prepare the food when it is ready to harvest.

Let's Get Writing (W)

Big Idea: Encourage your students to develop original skits

Supplies Needed: paper, pencils

Age Level: middle school or high school

If you want to add pizzazz to your youth worship experience, invite your teenagers to write skits. You probably have some budding playwrights in your midst who would enjoy creating scripts. A skit can be funny, poignant, or dramatic—just get your teenagers involved. Skits can add a new dimension to your services, and they can speak to teenagers' emotions or the challenges they are facing. Skits on pop culture or school are popular, and they can effectively illustrate biblical principles you'd like to communicate.

And, of course, once your teenagers have written skits, you'll need to find student actors. Your skit writers may want to play certain roles, or you may have the opportunity to get other young people involved in this new ministry.

KEY

(A) Activity   (G) Games   (S) Support

(C) Camp/Retreats   (I) Icebreaker   (T) Teaching

(F) Food   (M) Missions/Outreach   (W) Worship

Listen to the Radio ⓦ

Big Idea: Tune into the airwaves when you need some worship music

Supplies Needed: radio, sound system

Age Level: middle school or high school

You probably have a Christian radio station in your area—and if not, you can easily find an online radio station. If you're struggling to find musicians or you can't pay for the worship equipment you need, the radio might be an option for some free help.

Set up a nice sound system that can handle radio—either through a direct input or with a microphone—and bring your teenagers into a fun and engaging worship experience. Allow the radio to be your worship band; sing along to the music for a few songs before moving into a time of prayer, Scripture reading, and a message.

If you're listening to a station that takes requests, call in and ask for a favorite song to be played. Your teenagers might find themselves dancing or clapping along to a dynamic tune.

Look at Me! (T)

Big Idea: Learn to love yourself

Key Bible Verses: 1 Corinthians 13

Supplies Needed: hand mirror, Bible, index cards, pencils

Lesson Length: 15 minutes

Age Level: middle school

Bring the group into a circle, and read aloud 1 Corinthians 13 (the "love chapter"). Ask your teenagers to pay special attention to the Apostle Paul's closing comments about looking in a mirror and being fully known.

After you've read the Scripture, pass the mirror around the circle, and ask your students to take five to ten seconds to study their reflection in the mirror. Distribute the index cards and pencils and ask the teenagers to write down three things they love about themselves, such as appearance, personality, attitude, talents, and passions.

Then ask:

- Why do you think the Apostle Paul spoke of love as being greater than faith or hope?

- Do you find it easier to love yourself or to love others? Explain your answer.

- What are some of the reasons we may find it difficult to love ourselves? Why is it sometimes tough to love others?

Tell your teenagers they don't have to read what they wrote on their index cards, but you do want to ask a few questions:

- What did you learn by looking in the mirror and reflecting on the things you love about yourself?

KEY

 Activity   Games   Support

 Camp/Retreats   Icebreaker   Teaching

 Food    Missions/Outreach   Worship

- Do you believe God knows you even more deeply than you know yourself? Explain your answer.

- Do you believe God loves you more than you love yourself? Explain your perspective.

Close the session with prayer.

Lucky Seven Tag ⓖ ⓒ

Big Idea: Explore variations of a classic game

Supplies Needed: blindfolds, plastic hoops, flags or strips of bright cloth (depending on the specific game)

Age Level: middle school

Got some open space that works well for a game of Tag? Go for it. But the traditional Tag game won't hold your teenagers' imaginations for very long. Here are seven alternative versions of Tag; try one or try them all. Keep the game interesting.

Blob Tag

Begin with one person being "It." As this individual tags people, everyone who is tagged must join hands with "It," forming a growing blob of people pursuing others. The blob can become quite large and intimidating. Last person standing becomes the new "It" for the next round.

Marco Polo Tag

Of course, this one can be played in a swimming pool. The person who is "It" closes his or her eyes and says "Marco." Others in the pool must respond "Polo." With eyes still closed, "It" attempts to tag someone else, who then becomes the new "It."

But you can also play a version of this on land. Blindfold "It." Same rules apply.

Secret Person Tag

Before the game begins, designate a person in the youth group to be the "secret person." Tell your teenagers that play does not end until the secret person is tagged. Select someone to be "It" using the standard method. "It" must tag people until the secret person is tagged, at which point play ends, and the secret person can receive a prize, if you wish.

Teenagers vs. Adult Leaders

Adult leaders can challenge your teenagers to a competitive game of Tag. It's best if you have the same numbers of adult leaders and teenagers. Adult leaders try to tag teenagers. Teenagers try to tag adult leaders. The last person not to be tagged wins for that team.

Hula Hoop Tag

A fun alternative Tag incorporates plastic hoops. Spread a few hoops at various places on the ground. The hoops are safe zones where people cannot be tagged. The idea is to run between the safe havens without getting tagged. Set a time limit on how long people can stay in the safe zones, and make sure you have plenty of space between the hoops.

Flag Tag

This idea combines Flag Football and Tag. Everyone wears a flag in the belt (long pieces of bright cloth also work). "It" attempts to pull the flag from someone's belt. That person then becomes "It."

Tandem Tag

This works the same as traditional Tag, but everyone has a partner, including "It." Partners must hold hands and attempt to tag or elude other pairs.

Mission Box ⓢ

Big Idea: Offer a simple way for people to support your ministry

Supplies Needed: small security box

Age Level: high school

This simple tool is an ongoing project that can net small but consistent amounts of money over time. If you have someone in your congregation who is a craftsman or woodworker, ask if this person could construct a small security box that can be placed in a high-traffic area of your congregation. This little mission box should have a slot allowing people to donate bills or coins. The box can be identified with a youth mission project or a specific need that will enhance your ministry's effectiveness. You don't necessarily have to call attention to the box if it is located in a good, visible spot.

Some churches have used a variation of this idea: a portable box that can be placed on a tabletop at church functions or dinners, with an invitation for donations. Other congregations and youth groups have also successfully used the proverbial piggy bank.

Even from a small box, large support can emerge. Don't overlook the little things in making big things happen for God.

Money Matters (T) (G)

Big Idea: Discover that biblical stewardship is no game

Key Bible Verses: Luke 16:13; Hebrews 13:5

Supplies Needed: Bibles, paper, pencils, whiteboard, markers, Monopoly® game (several copies if you have a larger group)

Lesson Length: 90 minutes

Age Level: high school

This learning game helps teach personal stewardship, budgeting, and the faithful use of money. Begin by inviting your students to play a round of Monopoly®. Set up multiple games, if possible. Depending on the size of your group and how quickly the games progress, you may need to end the games at a predetermined time. Following the games, ask these questions:

- What does Monopoly® teach us about the use or misuse of money?

- What are some of the ways Monopoly® offers a realistic reflection of saving and spending habits? What are some of the ways the game is not realistic?

- If you could include some new elements to the game of Monopoly® that might reflect your personal experience with money, what would you add and why?

After the discussion, say something like: "The game of Monopoly® is a fun way of exploring the financial stresses of living on a budget. Perhaps some of you purchased too many properties to begin, or perhaps others tried to complete the game by hoarding your cash. Now, let's turn to the Bible and see if we can find some wisdom on how to use money wisely."

KEY

(A) Activity   (G) Games   (S) Support

(C) Camp/Retreats   (I) Icebreaker   (T) Teaching

(F) Food   (M) Missions/Outreach   (W) Worship

Read aloud Luke 16:13 and Hebrews 13:5. Then ask:

- What do these passages teach about money and faith?

- Why do many people struggle to trust God with their daily needs?

- How can we overcome that struggle?

Distribute the paper and pencils. On the whiteboard, write down the following list of items: clothing, food, rent (mortgage), car payment, entertainment, tuition, charitable giving, utilities, savings, and insurance. Add other items that you believe should be on the list.

Next, divide the students into two groups. Tell one group that it has $6,000 per month in income. Tell the other group it has $2,000 per month in income. Then ask each group to create a realistic budget (using the whiteboard items) for the monthly income. Allow 10 minutes to complete this task. (If you have a larger group of students, form more groups, but be sure to give yourself enough time for each group to report on its choices.)

Invite each group to share its budget with the group, and then ask these questions:

- What differences did you see between the budgets?

- Be honest here: Did any of you think about the verses I read earlier when you were making your decisions? Why or why not?

- Do you think your budget reflects actual living costs? Explain your answer.

- What have you learned today about making budgets and using money? How is this process easy and how is it difficult?

- What have you learned about how our values and choices about money shape our lives?

Read aloud the two Scripture passages again (Luke 16:13; Hebrews 13:5). Then ask:

- What new insights about finances and budgeting crossed your mind as you heard these Scripture verses again?

• How can God shape us spiritually through our use of money?

Close with a group prayer for God's guidance.

Monthly Birthday Party

Big Idea: Honor students and help them connect with others

Supplies Needed: cake or cupcakes, simple birthday cards

Age Level: middle school or high school

Add festiveness to your ministry by hosting a monthly birthday party for your students. Honor all the teenagers with birthdays in that particular month, and provide some simple birthday cards for the group to sign. Serve a simple cake with candles or cupcakes with individual candles.

Your monthly birthday parties are great ways to reconnect with teenagers who've drifted away from your group or those who haven't yet made a connection, so make sure you invite all of the teenagers in your church each month. The parties also can take the place of a more expensive meal if you're working with a tight budget. And it's a fun way to recruit new adult leaders or provide a service opportunity for some of the wonderful cooks in your church.

KEY

 Activity   Games   Support

 Camp/Retreats   Icebreaker    Teaching

 Food    Missions/Outreach   Worship

Monthly Meals (F)

Big Idea: Reduce costs by skipping weekly youth meals

Supplies Needed: pitch-in/potluck food, special decorative supplies

Age Level: middle school or high school

If you are having difficulty providing food for weekly youth meetings, switch to a monthly meal schedule. But add some touches that will make this monthly meal a bit special: tablecloths, real plates, and silverware.

Each student or family could bring food to this meal, or you could work up two or three menus where a $5 entrée is the center of a pitch-in meal. Having a monthly meal instead of a weekly one may also make your table time and conversations more special.

My Creed (T)

Big Idea: Encourage students to reflect on what they believe

Supplies Needed: paper, pencils

Lesson Length: 30 minutes

Age Level: middle school or high school

Begin the lesson by saying something like: "The word creed literally means, 'I believe.' We all live by one form of creed or another, even if the creed isn't written down. We all choose to follow a particular belief system that shapes our values and goals and decisions. Today we will consider what we believe, and why. You'll have the chance to create your personal statement of belief."

Distribute paper and pencil to each teenager. Offer the following four statements for your students to complete.

Then ask them to write a personal belief statement or creed based on their responses.

- The belief I hold most strongly is_____
- The values I hold most dear are_____
- I would describe myself as being_____
- What I hope to do for others involves_____

Once the teenagers have written their creeds, invite them to share these aloud. Post the creeds on a youth ministry wall, or ask the students to take their creeds home and put them in a visible spot. Challenge the teenagers to live by their creeds and to use their personal statements of belief as reminders of why they want to continue growing in their relationship with Jesus.

If your students need a little nudge to get them going, consider sharing the Apostle's Creed with them.

The Apostles' Creed (Traditional)

I believe in God the Father Almighty, maker of heaven and earth;

And in Jesus Christ his only Son our Lord:

Who was conceived by the Holy Spirit, born of the Virgin Mary, suffered under Pontius Pilate, was crucified, dead, and buried. He descended into Hell. The third day he rose from the dead; he ascended into heaven, and sitteth at the right hand of God the Father Almighty; from thence he shall come to judge the quick and the dead.

I believe in the Holy Spirit, the holy catholic church, the communion of saints, the forgiveness of sins, the resurrection of the body, and the life everlasting. Amen.

KEY

 Activity   Games   Support

 Camp/Retreats   Icebreaker   Teaching

 Food    Missions/Outreach   Worship

My Favorite Concert

Big Idea: Relive a favorite Christian concert on DVD

Supplies Needed: students' DVDs, DVD player

Age Level: middle school or high school

Many teenagers in your youth ministry have probably attended a large
Christian music festival or concert. They may have T-shirts, memorabilia,
and even DVDs from these concerts. Ask your teenagers to bring in
DVDs of their favorite Christian concerts or artists performing live. Show
the DVDs, and make your own mini-concert inside your youth room.
Encourage students to bring picnic blankets or lawn chairs, and provide
popcorn and sodas for the crowd.

My First Dollar

Big Idea: Create a fun environment of reminiscing and giving

Supplies Needed: letters from church members

Age Level: high school

Invite the people in your congregation to write brief letters to the youth
group describing how they made their "first dollar." Along with the letters,
ask the people to send along dollar bills (or perhaps encourage them to
send an amount equal to what they think that first dollar would be worth in
today's economy.)

Collect these letters, read them to the teenagers during a youth service
or in another group setting, and celebrate what God has done through
the businesses and work of your people. After reading all the letters, you
might identify one or two people who could share their stories personally
with your teenagers. You'll be doubly blessed because you'll also end up

with money to support your youth ministry's efforts, and some of the gifts may astound you.

This fundraiser can get the entire congregation involved—especially some of your older, successful members who would love to share their stories.

Mystery Worship Destination

Big Idea: Travel to an alternative worship site

Supplies Needed: $5 in gas money, vehicles, chaperones

Age Level: middle school or high school

Publicize your mystery destination a few weeks in advance and build up the intrigue and anticipation. Create a "mysterious" video to promote the trip during your youth services. Offer vague clues and hints about your destination. Do whatever it takes to convince your teenagers to participate in this "don't miss" experience.

Make sure you have enough vehicles and adult chaperones for your trip. Then do it! And don't forget—you are not going far. You only have $5 for gas, so think about a destination within a 10- to 15-mile radius of your church.

Once you arrive at your mystery destination, have a brief time of worship with your students, or provide a worship experience for the people at the destination.

Here are some popular mystery destination ideas you could consider.

- Local tourist destination (waterfall, overlook, historic home, or something similar)

- Beach

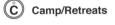
 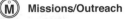

- City or state park

- Mall

- Restaurant (a dedicated party room is great)

- Movie theater

- Football field or gymnasium

- Jail parking lot

- Ranch or farm that provides horse riding

- Short hiking trail up a mountain

- Retreat center or campground

- Cabin or lodge

New Songs, New Leaders

Big Idea: Develop and expand your student worship teams

Supplies Needed: none

Age Level: high school

Tough times present us with opportunities to teach a "new song" and to train new leaders. This could be the season for bringing younger musicians forward to train, instruct, and encourage them. How about training a new, young musician on drums or keyboard? How about starting a new band from scratch and seeing where God leads?

During tough times, don't just sit and wait for the tide to turn—create a new venture, a new vision, a new path to the future. You'll be opening the door to new ministry opportunities for your teenagers and helping them realize they can use their skills, talents, and gifts to honor God today— they don't have to wait until they're adults.

Nine Square

Big Idea: Set your sights higher than just four squares

Supplies Needed: duct tape, chalk line, bouncy ball

Age Level: middle school or high school

Many children play Four Square at school on the playground, but you can upgrade this traditional game by creating your own Nine Square court. The court should consist of nine squares (each square measuring 5x5 feet). One person stands in each square, and the game is then played like traditional Four Square, with the center person playing the role of the server.

All you need are a chalk line and some duct tape to create your court, and a bouncy ball for play, and you're in business.

This game will probably become a popular one with your group, and some of your teenagers may even want to make a more permanent Nine Square court if you have space on an asphalt or concrete pad.

KEY

 Activity Games Support

 Camp/Retreats Icebreaker Teaching

 Food  Missions/Outreach Worship

Object Lesson Worship (W)

Big Idea: Help teenagers use ordinary items for great learning moments

Supplies Needed: student object lessons

Age Level: middle school

Invite some of your teenagers to create object-lesson talks to share in a youth worship service. These object lessons can be based upon items that the teenagers cherish or ones that have particular meaning or significance to them.

If the teenagers need help getting started or need some ideas to get their creative juices flowing, offer them this set of questions:

- What objects at home mean a lot to me? Why are they so meaningful?

- What could I say about an object to teach a lesson about my faith or about living a faithful life?

- What object might be unique enough to capture my friends' interest?

- What Bible verse comes to mind when I think about this object?

- How does the object work? How is its function similar to the way God might work in my life or in the world?

- What object would I like others to enjoy? Why? What can I say about that?

- What place does God have in my talk?

- How can I illustrate my talk with a story? What is the story?

Origami Table Décor (S) (A)

Big Idea: Transform paper into imaginative decorations

Supplies Needed: Origami paper and instruction book

Age Level: middle school or high school

You can accomplish this simple fundraiser during a single youth meeting. All you need are Origami paper (look online at orientaltrading.com for some $5 options), an Origami instruction book, and an hour or two to give your teenagers the chance to try their hand at making some of these paper creations.

Even a group of inexperienced teenagers can usually turn out a few dozen creations in an hour. They can sell them to people to use at parties, on their office desks, or just as table decorations at home. It's paper. It's folding. It's fun and teachable.

Parents Day Out—at Christmas (M)

Big Idea: Give parents a break by caring for their kids

Supplies Needed: DVDs, board games, inexpensive crafts, a few adult helpers

Age Level: high school

Reach out to your community at Christmas by providing a child care event for parents who need extra time for Christmas shopping and planning. Parents can bring their children to your church for this daytime or evening event and then use that time for holiday errands.

KEY

 Activity

 Games

 Support

 Camp/Retreats

 **Icebreaker**

 Teaching

 Food

 Missions/Outreach

 Worship

Your ministry can advertise this event by placing fliers around town (retail stores, Laundromats, grocery stores, and so on). Your teenagers can organize this event rather easily, with a few adult helpers on hand. Offer a variety of activities for the children, including board games, Christmas movies on DVD, and inexpensive crafts.

This event is principally an outreach to the community, but you'll probably have families from your congregation who will participate. Some parents might also feel moved to leave tips or contributions for the youth group.

Make sure you have release and emergency contact forms available for parents to fill out. Your children's ministry may have this information for families connected to your church, but the safest strategy is to have all parents or guardians complete the forms when they bring the kids to your event.

Partners in Service

Big Idea: Work with local agencies to meet nearby needs

Supplies Needed: phone book, phone

Age Level: high school

If you are looking for new ventures in mission (people, places, and situations that need your help and faith), don't try to figure out the needs by yourself. Turn to your local nonprofit agencies and social organizations. They can help you discover dozens of opportunities to minister in your county, no matter where you live.

During the time when many congregations were sending large work teams to help churches and communities affected by Hurricane Katrina, the Midwest was also experiencing enormous flooding.

Rather than sending work teams south, at great expense and organizational people-power, many Midwest congregations stayed local and rallied resources and strength to meet the needs of their more immediate neighbors.

But how did they find the people who most needed help? The answer was always just a phone call away. By calling the township trustees office, the local police, or the county social agencies, these congregations were quickly able to obtain names of families in need. No one had to travel far; for many churches, it only took a few dollars of gas to reach their destinations. And the families that received help were just as needy— and in some cases, even more so—as the people who lived a thousand miles away.

Maximize your mission efforts by responding to needs right where you are. Put some gas in the tank, drive into your community, and you've entered the mission field.

Phone Book Follies

Big Idea: Let your fingers do the walking to find some fun

Supplies Needed: phone books, paper, pencils

Age Level: middle school

Looking for a quick activity to help pass the time or fill an unexpected gap in the schedule? Use the local phone book or Yellow Pages to create a quick mental activity or group endeavor. If you are in a motel, this is an easy find, but you should be able to procure a phone book in most locations. Here are quick and fun ways to get the teenagers involved in phone book follies.

KEY

(A) Activity	(G) Games	(S) Support
(C) Camp/Retreats	(I) Icebreaker	(T) Teaching
(F) Food	(M) Missions/Outreach	(W) Worship

The Phone Book Scavenger Hunt

Prepare for this activity by perusing the phone book in advance. Write down a number of items (names, advertisements, phrases, pictures, and so on) that your teenagers can attempt to find by looking through the phone book. You should be able to create a scavenger hunt in just a few minutes. Give your students paper and pencil to keep track of the list. Set a time limit and keep the game moving.

The Name Game

Here's a fun game for a road trip. Distribute a few phone books, divide the students into teams of two to four people, and ask each team to find the funniest name listed in the phone book. Over the years the teenagers in my groups have discovered some really funny names. Ivan Von Eggcream is one that comes to mind—no kidding! You'll be surprised at the fun you can have with this one.

Feats of Strength

You've probably read about people who can tear a phone book in half, but have you ever tried? Don't do this one unless you have some old phone books, but if you can gather some outdated books, it's fun to let some of the macho kids in the group give it a try. There is actually a secret to tearing a phone book in half—but I'm not revealing it here! I like impressing other people with this one.

The Funny Ad

If you have Yellow Pages, divide the students into teams, and see which team can discover the funniest or strangest ad. Your teenagers will find plenty of candidates! You can easily do this game on a bus, so it's a fun travel activity.

Pick One (T) (i)

Big Idea: Let your teenagers choose the topic

Key Bible Verses: varies

Supplies Needed: photocopies of **"It's Optional!" handout (p. 174)**, Bibles, paper, scissors, pencils, tape (depending on the specific option)

Lesson Length: 30 minutes

Age Level: middle school

Give up control. Let your teenagers call the shots this time around. Instead of choosing this week's teaching topic, give your students several options. You'll enjoy this simple yet effective experience if you work with a group of finicky teenagers.

Photocopy the "It's Optional" handout (p. 174) and give a copy to each teenager. Be aware that Option 3 makes an effective icebreaker. Have pencils, scissors, and tape available. Ask your group to choose one of the options, and follow the instructions for that particular option.

KEY

 (A) Activity   (G) Games   (S) Support

(C) Camp/Retreats   (i) Icebreaker   (T) Teaching

(F) Food   (M) Missions/Outreach   (W) Worship

Pray It Up Ⓜ Ⓣ

Big Idea: Prepare your teenagers for the next mission opportunity

Key Bible Verses: Matthew 28:16-20

Supplies Needed: Bible, travel bag, cross

Length: 20 minutes (for teaching element)

Age Level: high school

Build excitement and momentum toward your next mission trip by focusing on the various missions or the missionaries your church currently supports. For example, your youth ministry could

- Create a bulletin board or display featuring your congregation's current and recent mission and outreach efforts.

- Create a display featuring the various missionaries and families your congregation supports.

- Create a thermometer chart showing the growth of the youth mission fund for your next trip.

Consider preparing the students for mission involvement through this Bible lesson. You'll need a travel bag with a cross inside of it and a Bible. Invite the teenagers to sit in a circle, and place the travel bag in the middle. Ask this question:

- What items would you normally place in a travel bag if you were going on a trip?

After your teenagers have named a number of items, read aloud from Matthew 28:16-20. Then ask these questions:

- What is the core of the mission that Jesus wants his disciples to fulfill?

- How has that mission changed in the 2,000 years since Jesus walked the face of the earth?

- Do you think God is still asking people to go into the world to spread the good news of Jesus through word and deed? Explain your answer.

Following your discussion, open the travel bag and take out the cross. Sit it in the middle of the circle and ask:

- How is taking a trip with Jesus different from other trips? What are some similarities?

- What type of work could we do to fulfill Jesus' call to go into the world?

- Where might we find some of these needs nearby? Where would we find them in places far away?

Following your discussion, ask the students for suggestions on possible mission projects and then close with prayer.

Pray the Directory

Big Idea: Intercede for people in your congregation

Supplies Needed: roster of congregational members

Age Level: middle school or high school

Prayer is always vital for Christians, but its importance seems more profound during tough times. One of the ways your teenagers can discover the power of prayer is by praying for others in your own congregation. This is a particularly dynamic worship experience for any church that is experiencing high unemployment among the membership or for a congregation that is facing other significant challenges.

KEY

 Activity   Games   Support

 Camp/Retreats   Icebreaker   Teaching

 Food   Missions/Outreach   Worship

Bring pictorial church directories to the youth meeting (or print directories of your congregation by family name). If your church has a privacy policy, you can likely still print family names in alphabetical order.

Divide your students into teams, and ask each small group to take a portion of the alphabet (such as names beginning with A-D, E-H, and so on). Invite the teenagers to pray silently or collectively for the families of the congregation.

As a guide, invite the youth to pray for families who may need

- Financial help

- Wisdom and guidance as they make big decisions

- More faith, hope, or joy in their households

- More mutual love and respect

Praying for the families of the congregation in this way is powerful, and you might want to inform the entire congregation of your prayers during your adult worship service or through your bulletin, newsletter, or e-mail. The congregation will appreciate the teenagers' prayers and the extra measure of support.

If your congregation is too large for teenagers to pray for each family individually, you could modify this idea and simply pray for all the teenagers of the church. A praying youth ministry will certainly find strength in prayer during tough times.

Pray the News

Big Idea: Remember global needs in prayer

Supplies Needed: newspapers, poster board

Age Level: middle school and high school

Get your teenagers thinking about their world by "praying the news." Bring in a stack of newspapers, and invite the youth to tear out one or two news stories that catch their attention or interest them. These stories may be local, national, or international in scope.

Tack up some of the stories, or glue them onto poster board. Divide the teenagers into groups of two or three for prayer and reflection on the news stories. Your students may also pray for situations, events, human needs, world leaders, or people or families whose lives have been devastated.

If you want to pray for these situations by using some specific Scripture readings, consider using these passages:

- Psalm 23 (The Lord is my shepherd)
- Psalm 46 (God is our refuge and strength)
- Matthew 5:43-48 (Love your enemies)
- Matthew 6:25-34 (Do not worry)
- Galatians 5:22-26 (The fruit of the Spirit)
- Philippians 2:1-11 (The attitude of Christ)
- 1 John 3:18-24 (Love one another)

KEY

 Activity

 Camp/Retreats

 Food

 Games

 Icebreaker

 Missions/Outreach

Support

Teaching

Worship

Prayer Wall

Big Idea: Devote some space for prayer needs

Supplies Needed: wall space, poster board, push pins

Age Level: middle school

Create a prayer wall to encourage your teenagers to pray for others. Use a bulletin board or other wall space where adults and teenagers in your congregation can post their prayer needs. People could also display photos of missionaries, family members, or friends who need healing, hope, or guidance. The prayer wall can become a tool you use to regularly pray for people in the congregation and in the youth ministry.

You could also use the wall to list the names of past youth directors, volunteers, adult leaders, or others who have helped shape your youth ministry. This is a wonderful way to recognize the contributions of foundational leaders, and it encourages your students to continue praying for these leaders and their ministries.

Progressive Fast-Food Dinner

Big Idea: Hit the road to find a $5 four-course meal

Supplies Needed: transportation

Age Level: middle school or high school

OK, so fast food isn't always the healthiest option, but maybe you and your teenagers deserve a break today. Mix food, folks, and fun with this progressive dinner. Invite each teenager to bring $5 for dinner, and using adult chaperones as drivers, hit up three or four fast-food restaurants. Instruct the teenagers to order "appetizers" at the first, "beverages" at the second, "main course" at the third, and "dessert" at the fourth.

Or if you want to eat fresh without the expense and time constraints of driving, have your adult helpers run for the border and pick up food from a variety of restaurants—and let that be your meal.

Increase the finger lickin' fun with "blind" taste tests of various hamburgers, fries, or desserts. Find out which teenagers have the sharpest taste buds. See? You can have it your way.

Progressive Food Drive

Big Idea: Gather donated items to feed your teenagers

Supplies Needed: donated canned and boxed goods

Age Level: middle school or high school

During tough times your church may reduce the food budget for your youth group. But if your teenagers are accustomed to eating when they get together, consider holding a progressive food drive.

Here's how it can work.

Make a list of items that the teenagers (or congregation members) can bring to meetings each week. Over the course of a month, you'll collect food items that can be turned into meals for the teenagers. Here are some suggestions:

Week 1
Bring canned vegetables and canned fruit.
Suggestions: green beans, corn, peas, peaches, pineapple, apricots

Week 2
Bring dried staples or soups.
Suggestions: rice, beans, cornbread mix, breakfast cereals, canned soup

Week 3

Bring canned meats or chicken nuggets.

Suggestions: chicken nuggets, tuna, chicken, mackerel

Week 4

Bring boxed mixes and frozen pizzas.

Suggestions: pizzas, Hamburger Helper®, Tuna Helper®, taco dinners, instant potatoes

Once you've collected the items, place one or two of the items from each category in a box to provide a complete meal for the youth group. And if your congregation responds with more food than your teenagers can consume, give away the excess to a local food bank.

Progressive Pocket Change ⓢ

Big Idea: Turn pennies and nickels into changed lives

Supplies Needed: student collectors and counters

Age Level: high school

Some years back a friend of mine used this unique concept to practically fund an entire mission trip in just one month. The larger your congregation is, the larger the potential for success. You'll need permission from your senior pastor or church board to do this fundraiser, but it works!

A couple of weeks before launching your Month of Pocket Change fundraiser, begin promoting this opportunity for church members to help fund the youth mission trip through their coin contributions. You'll do this month-long fundraiser over four progressive Sundays.

On the first Sunday, invite the congregation to bring pennies. You'll be amazed at how much you can collect from this first step alone. Many people have hundreds or thousands of pennies in jars and other containers. Invite them to give!

On the second Sunday, invite the congregation to bring in nickels. On the third Sunday, it's dimes. And on the fourth Sunday, we're talking quarters.

Make plans to have your teenagers count these coins, deposit them, and run the totals through your books or other protocol. With a bit of planning and generosity on the part of your church, this pocket-change month can yield some significant funds.

Be certain you don't do this one too often. Turning it into an annual event is probably even too much. Just know that when you do invite the congregation to bring in pocket change, people will respond.

Put a Psalm to Music

Big Idea: Use biblical lyrics to write new worship songs

Supplies Needed: Bibles, paper, pencils

Age Level: high school

The psalms have long been a lyrical source for songwriters. And you may be surprised to find that some of your teenagers can write great music, too. If you have some aspiring musicians in your group, guide them to some psalms that would make great music. For starters, consider these:

- Psalm 1
- Psalm 8
- Psalm 11
- Psalm 18 (This is a long psalm, but it includes dynamic imagery of God's strength, power, and provision.)

- Psalm 34:1-3
- Psalm 43
- Psalm 46
- Psalm 66
- Psalm 121
- Psalm 148

KEY

 **Activity**

 Games

 Support

Camp/Retreats **Icebreaker** **Teaching**

Food **Missions/Outreach** **Worship**

Random Acts (M)

Big Idea: Perform unexpected deeds in your hometown

Key Bible Verses: Luke 10:1-5

Supplies Needed: Bible, tools, $5 for gas money, chaperones

Age Level: high school

Capitalize on your passion for mission and outreach with this great mission project that is spontaneous and fun. Choose a day when your teenagers can devote several hours to mission work. Divide your students into teams, and travel via family vans, cars, or buses to various points in town. You don't have to go far, and $5 in gas money should cover your travel.

Before you leave your church grounds, gather the entire group together, and do the following:

- Read Luke 10:1-5.

- Discuss: Why do you think Jesus sent the disciples out in small groups instead of individually? What can we learn from this? What types of needs did the disciples expect to find? What types of needs can we expect to find in our town?

- Divide the group into teams and, if you like, provide some suggestions as to the type of random acts of kindness your group could perform for free.

- Here are 10 examples of random acts of kindness:

  1. Helping someone pump gas at a gas station

  2. Helping someone rake leaves or grass clippings

  3. Washing someone's car

  4. Washing someone's car windows

  5. Washing the exterior windows of someone's home

6. Straightening a bent mailbox

7. Cleaning a roadside or gutter near someone's home

8. Paying someone's toll at a toll booth

9. Paying for someone's french fries at a restaurant

10. Opening the door for people at a busy store or restaurant

Once you have established a plan for the day and a time limit for the project, disperse into the community. Provide tools as necessary. Make sure you have sufficient adult chaperones for driving and supervising each small group. And if you like, provide some information about your youth group or your church (worship times, special ministries, or upcoming events) in a small brochure that you can hand out after the groups perform their random acts of kindness.

Once everyone has returned to the church, talk about the projects. Invite the teenagers to discuss their experiences. The following questions can guide you:

- How did people respond to your offer to perform random acts of kindness? Did they assume there was some kind of "catch"? Share one of your stories.

- Did you have any surprising conversations with people? Share the details.

- What was the most challenging situation you experienced today?

- What was it like to do mission work among people who are your friends and neighbors?

- After reading Luke 10:1-5 again, ask: What new insights do you have now about the mission Jesus is calling us to fulfill?

- How will today's experience affect your faith?

KEY

 Activity

 Camp/Retreats

Food

 Games

Icebreaker

Missions/Outreach

 Support

Teaching

Worship

Your teenagers will probably ask you to repeat this mission event every year—and the cost is minimal while the results are enormous.

Read the Label

Big Idea: Test teenagers' memories by examining food labels

Supplies Needed: canned and boxed foods, paper, pencils

Age Level: middle school and high school

Here's a fun food game you can use during one of those rainy days when bad weather spoils your outdoor plans. Gather several canned or boxed food items. Choose food that teenagers can easily consume at the end of the activity. Bring the students together in a circle, and pass each product around the group as you say something like this: "Study the nutrition facts panel on each food item. After you have taken a few moments, pass the item to your neighbor."

After each item has traveled once around the circle, distribute pencils and paper to each student. Then say something like: "I'm now going to test your memory. I will mention each food product, one at a time. As I do, think about what you read on the nutrition labels, and write down the amount of carbohydrates, sodium, and calories in a serving for that product."

Play in teams or as individuals. See who has the best "food sense." After you have learned about the nutrition, eat the food that you just discussed.

Rope a Dope (G)

Big Idea: Discover games that require nothing but a rope

Supplies Needed: ropes, stopwatch, orange plastic cone, blindfolds (depending on the game)

Age Level: middle school or high school

If you have a 10-foot rope, here are some easy games you can quickly organize. If you don't have a rope, you can purchase one at a hardware store for just a few bucks. Clothesline rope would also work for a few of these games.

All Knotted Up
Tie seven simple knots in the rope. Divide the youth group into two teams. Using a stopwatch or clock, see how quickly the first team can untie the knots. Retie the knots, and then time the second team. You could also play this game by allowing individuals to compete or as a relay game, with team members untying one knot at a time before passing the rope to the next team member.

Lasso
Form the rope into a simple lasso. Place an orange plastic cone a few feet away. See which teenager can lasso the cone the most times in one minute.

Rope Pull
Place several small, lightweight objects on the floor or ground. Divide your teenagers into two teams. See which team can use the rope (tossing it and pulling it back) to capture the most objects or pull the objects to a designated spot. The teenagers can only touch the objects with the rope. This one is rather crazy and forces the students to work together to solve a problem.

Design

Divide the young people into teams, and see which team can create the most intricate rope design without tying the rope into a knot. Teams may only place the rope on the floor or ground in a pattern. Longer rope works best for this activity.

Squared Off

Everyone will need to be blindfolded. Form a circle, with everyone holding on to the rope. Ask the teenagers to remain standing and work together to form the rope into a square. After the students believe they've formed a square, have them place the rope on the ground. The teenagers may then remove their blindfolds to see how well they have worked together to form the square.

Scrap Your Plans ⓢ

Big Idea: Facilitate creativity for scrapbooking aficionados

Supplies Needed: construction paper, stickers

Age Level: middle school and high school

Scrapbooking has become a hobby for millions of people, and your youth group can turn this relaxing pastime into a venture that funds ministry. Begin by creating scrapbooking supplies out of construction paper, blank stickers, and other useable items. Purchase a few scrapbook supplies at a discount store and have these on hand, too.

Then set up a scrapbooking afternoon or evening. Make sure the people who come to the event know they can purchase some of their scrapbooking supplies from the youth group. Have enough materials on hand for a decent selection.

Or instead of selling the supplies, your youth ministry could rent out table space. Give each individual a card table or folding table dedicated for his or her use for the scrapbooking event. Many will also make a donation.

Secret Partners (S)

Big Idea: Invest anonymously in your teenagers' spiritual lives

Supplies Needed: a list of youth group members or ministry needs

Key Bible Verse: Matthew 6:3-4

If you have a smaller youth group or you'd like to fund some aspect of your ministry through personal involvement, try Secret Partners. Here's how it works. Make a list of the teenagers in your group, a list of the items you need for a ministry, or a list of specific ministry goals. Invite people in the congregation to consider becoming "secret partners" to come alongside the youth and support them or the ministry through their gifts.

For a biblical foundation, use Matthew 6:3-4: "But when you give to someone in need, don't let your left hand know what your right hand is doing. Give your gifts in private, and your Father, who sees everything, will reward you."

I've used this idea at various times, and I've seen some terrific secret partners come alongside the teenagers. But of course, I don't know who the partners are. They are secret partners, after all.

KEY

(A) Activity   (G) Games   (S) Support

(C) Camp/Retreats   (I) Icebreaker   (T) Teaching

(F) Food   (M) Missions/Outreach   (W) Worship

Sell the Recipes (S) (F)

Big Idea: Cook and serve homemade soups to support your teenagers

Supplies Needed: homemade soups, recipe cards, $5 for crackers

Age Level: middle school or high school

Some of the best cooks in your congregation probably have some hearty soup recipes they'd be willing to share. Schedule a soup night, and then invite some of these top chefs to prepare a pot of their favorite soup as a fundraiser. Also ask them for permission to print their soup recipes on a few cards.

At the soup night, the teenagers can serve as hosts and hostesses, serve up the soup for a freewill offering or for a certain amount per bowl, and sell the recipe cards for a dollar each. This idea is tasty and fun, and it should net the youth group some nice fundraising money, too.

And be sure you seed the event by purchasing $5 worth of crackers.

Show or Tell? (M)

Big Idea: Examine mission opportunities for your teenagers

Supplies Needed: pencils, photocopies of the **"Step Out and Serve" handout (p. 175)**

Age Level: middle school and high school

Perhaps you've heard this saying: "I'd rather see a sermon than hear one." Indeed, there's nothing more exciting than outreach with "shoe leather" invested in it!

We are most effective as Christ-followers when we are on the move, rather than sedentary, chair-sitting, thought-processing believers.

I recently heard a stand-up comic put it this way: "My grandmother has been going to Bible study for 35 years. I keep wondering…when is she going to take the test?" Sooner or later we must step out in mission and service. We must put our faith into action, letting our minds and hearts become feet and hands.

To get started on your mission and outreach during tough times (whether economic, disaster-related, or extreme circumstances) give your teenagers and adult leaders an opportunity to become involved in new ways. Use this little handout to quickly assess the mission your group can do on a shoestring budget. Don't waste time trying to reinvent the past or dream of what once was. Get going on God's plan for tomorrow.

Soup's On

Big Idea: Dish up some warmth for needy families

Supplies Needed: soup or sandwiches

Age Level: middle school or high school

Even if your church isn't located in the inner city or doesn't have a large homeless population nearby, you can still do a soup event that helps low-income families in your community (and yes, they are there).

Call some of the social agencies and social workers in your town or county. You may also wish to contact women's shelters, the police department, your school district, and even some of the service clubs in your town. Inform them about your "soup dinner" and give a time and location, with the invitation that anyone in need may attend. You don't necessarily have to hold the meal at your church; you might be able to convince the people in charge of a community center, a park, or even a town hall to donate the space for this event.

KEY

 Activity   Games   Support

 Camp/Retreats   Icebreaker   Teaching

 Food   Missions/Outreach   Worship

Arrange for your teenagers and some of the cooks in your congregation to prepare the soup dinner (various soups, crackers, breads, vegetables, and desserts make a great menu). Bring in the food, open the doors, and let people warm up over a hot bowl and some good conversation. As a summer or spring alternative to soup, make sandwiches instead. Sub sandwiches work well, and you can turn to the same groups for help in preparation and promotion.

You'll meet some new friends through this outreach, and you'll be demonstrating the love of Jesus in a tangible and meaningful way. Food is the gateway to the heart. And your mission of soup can be a meaningful outreach in your community.

Spring Clean Brigade

Big Idea: Serve your community by cleaning homes

Supplies: tools, $5 of cleaning supplies

Age Level: middle school or high school

Remember when your grandmother used to do spring-cleaning? Well, maybe not. But your teenagers can turn the spring-cleaning ritual into a unique outreach in your community. Get organized with some simple cleaning supplies like brushes, squeegees, paper towels, ammonia, mops, and brooms. Create a flier that you can distribute around your community advertising your Spring Clean Brigade.

With help from adult chaperones, take your brigade to the community and demonstrate your mission heart. This may sound trite, but it's true: You don't have to travel far to meet a need.

A spring-cleaning mission can include any or all of the following services:

Interior	**Exterior**
Washing windows	Washing windows
Sweeping floors	Cleaning gutters
Mopping tile/hardwood floors	Hosing off siding
Vacuuming carpet	Preparing flower beds
Cleaning sinks/bathtubs	Rinsing window screens
Dusting	Hosing a deck
Washing baseboards	Adjusting windows and doors

Summer Hockey

Big Idea: Use ice chunks to play parking-lot hockey

Supplies Needed: 10 brooms, ice chunks, ice chest, orange marker cones

Age Level: high school

If you have an open parking lot and a desire to cool down during the hot days of summer, try a game of summer hockey. You'll need a couple of makeshift goals (orange cones for markers will do just fine), brooms for 10 players, and several large chunks of ice (five- to seven-inch squares work best) that can be stored in an ice chest. If you can't find ice that size, you may consider chiseling smaller pieces this size out of a larger ice block.

KEY

 Activity   Games   Support

 Camp/Retreats   Icebreaker   Teaching

 Food   Missions/Outreach   Worship

Divide the group into two teams—five per team, without goalies. Distribute the brooms, and see which team can score more goals by "brooming" a piece of ice around the hot parking lot into the goal.

These large pieces of ice will slide around very easily on the hot surface—but they will melt quickly, so have plenty of extra "pucks" on hand.

During breaks from the game, cool off with some shaved-ice or snow-cone refreshment.

Support the Unemployed (M)

Big Idea: Find ways to help people who are searching for jobs

Age Level: middle school or high school

Your teenagers can be a source of encouragement, inspiration, and assistance to people who are out of work. There are many ways to help. For example:

- Create a bulletin board or posting area for job openings and clippings from the newspapers.

- Your teenagers could provide child care on certain days for people who need time to write a job resume or go to a job interview.

- Students could assemble kits for families enduring the effects of unemployment. The kits could contain simple toiletries like detergent, soap, and toothpaste. Often, these staples are some of the most needed items. The kits could be expanded to include snack items, paper, pens, paper clips, and perhaps a calendar and organizer.

The teenagers could work with the pastoral staff to create volunteer positions at the church to provide meaningful involvement for people searching for full-time jobs. Every church needs help clearing sidewalks, raking, mowing, mopping, dusting, and even polishing pews and brass work.

These tasks can be meaningful to people who want to serve God during their unemployment.

The teenagers could create an "intercession hotline." People who desire prayer can ask the young people to lift them up daily or weekly. The hotline could be set up on the church website or as a drop box somewhere in the church with prayer cards.

Survivor Basics

Big Idea: Discover how God is our provider

Key Bible Verses: 1 Kings 17:8-16

Supplies Needed: Bible, index cards, pencils

Lesson Length: 20 Minutes

Age Level: high school

Ask the students to form a circle for this lesson. Give each teenager an index card and a pencil.

Say something like: "Take a few minutes to consider what you need to survive. Write down five things that would be important for your survival."

After five to seven minutes, invite one of the students to read aloud 1 Kings 17:8-16. Then ask:

- For just one moment, pretend that you are God in this story. What are some other ways you could have performed a miracle for this widow?

- Do you think Elijah had any doubts as he spoke the words recorded in verses 13 and 14? Explain your answer.

- What does this story teach you about life's necessities?

KEY

 Activity   Games   Support

 Camp/Retreats    Icebreaker   Teaching

 Food    Missions/Outreach   Worship

- What does this passage teach you about God's provision?

Invite several of the students to read their lists. **Then ask:**

- On an average day, are you aware of how God provides for you? How can you become more aware of God's daily provisions?

- What are some ways you've grown accustomed to relying on your own ingenuity and abilities instead of relying on God's ability to provide?

- What can you learn about God's provision when you go through tough times?

- Besides material things and "stuff," what are some other blessings God provides?

Close the lesson by offering a prayer for God's blessing and abundance, and pray for people who are unemployed or in need of God's strength.

Taking a Stand

Big Idea: Declare who you are and then make some new friends

Supplies Needed: paper, markers, tape

Age Level: middle school or high school

This activity requires movement and offers a great option for your group when you are forced indoors or when you want to learn more about one another. Before the activity, number five pieces of paper consecutively, from one to five. Post these papers at eye level, at spaced intervals along one wall.

Tell the teenagers that as you read the following statements, they should stand beside the number that best represents their opinions. The paper marked "1" represents "I don't like this" or "I disagree with this." The paper marked "5" represents "I love this" or "I agree with this."

Some statements may seem more "gray," and that's what the numbers in the middle of the scale represent.

- I would like to be a millionaire.

- I have no doubts or questions about God.

- I like anchovies on my pizza.

- I think my education is important.

- I would like to go on a mission trip to another country.

- I love to say "Dude!"

- If God wants me to be a pastor, I will do it.

- I like the idea of getting married.

- I like to read books.

- I am addicted to text messaging.

- I am certain Jesus has saved me.

- I love to pray.

- I like to read the Bible.

- I love to give money to God's work or to help others.

- I want to own a new car some day.

- I have big dreams for my life.

- Most days, I'm very happy.

- I have all the friends I need.

- God has helped me face a problem in the past year.

- I am ready for this activity to end.

KEY

(Â) Activity   (Ĝ) Games   (Ŝ) Support

(Ĉ) Camp/Retreats   (Î) Icebreaker   (T̂) Teaching

(F̂) Food   (M̂) Missions/Outreach   (Ŵ) Worship

Taste and See ⓣ

Big Idea: Appreciate God's goodness through the Lord's Supper

Key Bible Verses: Psalm 34:8; 1 Corinthians 11:23-26

Supplies Needed: Bible, cans of Spam®, forks, communion supplies

Lesson Length: 30 minutes

Age Level: middle school or high school

Start this lesson by encouraging—or daring—some of your youth or a few of your adult volunteers to sample the Spam® or attempt to eat a whole can. Afterward, read aloud Psalm 34:8: "Taste and see that the Lord is good."

Ask your teenagers these questions:

- How would you describe the taste of Spam®?

- Why do you think its taste provokes such strong emotions or reactions?

Talk about the Lord's Supper, and read aloud from 1 Corinthians 11:23-26. Then say something like: "The Lord's Supper is a sensory experience. For example, bread is something we can touch, taste, and smell. The bread invites us on many levels to experience God's grace and goodness. The same is true of the cup. We can taste how sweet God's goodness is."

Invite the teenagers to discuss other ways the bread and cup are sensory experiences, as well as spiritual ones. Then ask:

- How might your senses help you experience a spiritual awakening?

- How might your senses bring you closer to God?

Following discussion, partake of Communion together, and invite the teenagers to ask questions about Communion. If you're a volunteer leader, consider inviting one of your pastors to join you for this experience and to answer students' questions about Communion.

GAME IDEAS

These ideas can help any youth ministry create new games or re-create old ones that have been a part of the ministry for years. Adapt and expand them. Save money; have a blast.

1. X Games...Church Style

If you have a large parking area or an open space large enough to set up some cones, a small competition course, or a series of events, try holding your own weird but safe version of the X Games. Get some kneepads, elbow pads, and helmets, and bring in a few skateboards for some "soft" landing competition. (Have the teenagers bring these items in—don't purchase them!) Find a tricycle, and see who can navigate the cone course the fastest (watch the knees). Use a Slip 'n Slide on a slight decline and discover who can flop the farthest on the belly. Be creative! Your teenagers will have a blast!

2. The Game Guru

Yes, most congregations have a game guru. You know: that person with all the energy who can take a group of unruly teenagers and whip them into a gaming frenzy with nothing but an open field and a few instructions. The next time you take a retreat, travel to summer camp, or organize that small group outing, make sure you enlist the help of the Game Guru. Ask this person to create games that will keep your teenagers hopped up on adrenaline. A fanciful Game Guru can create a game in practically any environment and can work with very little. Yeah, you know who I'm talking about! You probably have that person in your church. Just ask.

3. Video Game Tournament

Check with a few of the guys in the youth group, and you can round up a supply of Xbox, Wii, and PlayStation systems. Maybe you've stashed away an old Nintendo or Atari system in your garage. A lot of your guys will love the idea of a video game tournament. This idea may not appeal to larger groups, but if you have a group of guys who are eager for entertainment, you don't have to spend much to have big fun.

4. Red Rubber Ball

What games can you play with a red rubber ball? Just about anything. If you want to put new zip in some old games, use a red rubber ball instead of a basketball, or substitute the red rubber ball for a soccer ball, a softball, or a flying disk to mix up the outcomes to traditional games. Don't buy new equipment; just throw this one into the mix.

5. World Record

Some years ago, when my wife and I were on vacation in Florida, we happened upon a beach that was swarming with teenagers. Hundreds of them. They were everywhere. Suddenly we noticed they were lining up along the beach, about as far as we could see. I asked one of the teenagers who they were and what they were trying to accomplish; I learned they were part of a Christian gathering, and they were attempting to set a world record for the longest conga line. OK.

Well, you may not have hundreds of teenagers in your group, but you can at least pretend to be setting a world record. Invite the students to dream up a few safe options for attempting a record. Or if you are not this adventurous, how about keeping track of your own "youth group records"? As the years go by, you could challenge other youth groups in town to try to best the records other groups have set—number of schools represented in your group, number of teenagers who own skateboards, number of students on mission trips, number of pounds of cans for recycling, number of girls named Britney in the group, and so on. You don't need a budget to do this one—just some crazy creativity.

Thanksgiving Dinner

Big Idea: Express your thanks by serving others

Supplies Needed: homemade or donated food

Age Level: high school

Make Thanksgiving a more meaningful holiday this year for your teenagers and your church families. Launch a community Thanksgiving meal to minister to individuals and families who may have few reasons to be thankful. A Thanksgiving meal will open your church doors to those in need, and it's a great opportunity for your church to demonstrate God's love. We represent Christ well when we are serving and caring.

To keep costs low for your Thanksgiving outreach, ask your church's families to provide a little extra food for others. Maybe they can cook two turkeys this year: one for the outreach and one for their own family. Talk with managers of grocery stores and retailers in your area to sponsor this dinner. Many will eagerly contribute toward the effort, and some may simply ask for a small token of advertising (such as a small sign that says "Turkey Generously Provided by _____").Thanksgiving can truly become a day of outreach and love, and your teenagers can be the primary servers and helpers.

And an added bonus: Everyone who serves will have a greater appreciation for Thanksgiving and a deeper sense of thankfulness for their blessings—especially the blessing of opening our hands to serve others.

KEY

(A) **Activity**   (G) **Games**   (S) **Support**

(C) **Camp/Retreats**   (I) **Icebreaker**   (T) **Teaching**

(F) **Food**   (M) **Missions/Outreach**   (W) **Worship**

Thinking of You (M)

Big Idea: Reach out to inactive and disconnected teenagers

Supplies Needed: $5 bag of assorted gifts

Age Level: middle school

Effectively reach out to teenagers who may feel disconnected or who have been absent from the youth group. Organize teams to personally deliver small gifts. These gifts don't have to be expensive or extravagant. Visit a dollar store, and see what you can find for $5. Or check out orientaltrading.com to find hundreds of less-than-$5 gift bags. You'll be surprised at the selection.

Include one or two personal notes from friends in the gift bag, along with a schedule of upcoming youth group activities.

Top Ten (A) (I)

Big Idea: Invite students to create their own top ten lists

Supplies Needed: paper, pencils

Age Level: middle school or high school

These days, it seems like everyone has a top ten list for something. So why not use the top ten list as a discussion starter?

Distribute paper and pencils, and choose one of the following topics to get your meeting off to a fun and energetic start.

- Top ten movies
- Top ten songs
- Top ten thoughts about God

- Top ten funniest moments

- Top ten goals in life

- Top ten places I'd like to visit

- Top ten favorite foods

- Top ten fears

- Top ten happiest moments

- Top ten favorite animals

Town and Country

Big Idea: Connect with new families in your community

Supplies Needed: brochures about your church or youth ministry

Age Level: high school

Get creative when looking for ways to get information about your youth ministry or church into the hands of new families in your community. With all of these methods, it's best to have nice brochures and accurate information about your youth ministry or church, as well as contact phone numbers and e-mail addresses for leaders. Here are some ways you could reach out to new families:

- Contact your local chamber of commerce and see if there is a Welcome Wagon business in your area. If so, call Welcome Wagon and ask about policies and methods for including your congregational information in the packets that are delivered to new residents.

KEY

 Activity   Games   Support

 Camp/Retreats   Icebreaker   Teaching

 Food   Missions/Outreach   Worship

- Check with real estate agencies. Many agents will include information about area churches in their community packets when families are shopping for a house. In fact, many families specifically ask about schools, sports, and churches when they move to a new city.

- Check with local hotels. Many of these businesses include information about local churches in their phone or desk directories. Be sure your congregation is included in this listing. Many new families may spend a night or two in a hotel when they are waiting for a house to close or when work is being done to prepare the home for move-in condition.

- Check newspaper listing for home foreclosures in your area. It's a sad situation, but your youth group can reach out to these families—even though they might be leaving your town or neighborhood—by sending along a care packet or a letter saying that you're praying for them and inviting them to attend worship, Bible studies, support groups, or youth meetings. Your outreach efforts will display the love of Christ to people going through tough times.

TP Basketball Ⓖ

Big Idea: Discover a new use for rolls of toilet paper

Supplies Needed: rolls of toilet paper

Age Level: middle school

If you have a basketball goal, a few rolls of toilet paper, and a group of teenagers with a sense of humor, try Toilet Paper Basketball. There's no "dribbling" in this game and no "dunking" or "swirlies" allowed, but your teenagers will enjoy this variation of basketball.

The rules are simple: Two teams, passing a roll of toilet paper to teammates, attempt to put the roll through the basket to score a goal.

There are two ways to play: You can "free spool" or make the rolls a bit more solid by placing a layer of duct tape around them. You can also spice up the game a bit by creating novelty shots (4-point shots or similar ideas) or special rules about how the teams can handle or pass the roll.

You can also play this game with a small group as a H-O-R-S-E basketball contest.

Travel Menu

Big Idea: Turn restaurant menus into travel entertainment

Supplies Needed: various restaurant menus

Age Level: middle school or high school

Before leaving on your trip or excursion, pick up a few paper takeout menus from some local restaurants (Chinese and Mexican menus often work best). Distribute the menus among the teenagers while traveling, and ask the teenagers to select one or two items from that particular menu that they would like to sample. Take a poll and see which menu items are the most popular.

Follow this up with a memory activity. Collect the menus and see how many teenagers can remember the prices for various dishes or if they can recall the names of some of the dishes if you read the ingredients aloud.

Menus make fine travel companions, and you can use this activity on the bus, at the airport, or between stops.

KEY

 Activity   Games   Support

 Camp/Retreats   Icebreaker   Teaching

 Food   Missions/Outreach   Worship

T-Shirt Friends Ⓐ Ⓒ

Big Idea: Tell them how much you care by writing on their shirts

Supplies Needed: fabric paints, hair dryer, plain white T-shirts (asks your teenagers to bring their own)

Age Level: middle school or high school

This fun activity will help your teenagers bond. Invite all the students to bring in a plain white T-shirt. Purchase $5 of fabric paints from a discount store like Hobby Lobby, and then invite the teenagers to create a "front" to their T-shirts—words, symbols, and drawings that represent who they are.

Allow these to dry (help the process along with a hair dryer). Then invite the teenagers to sign the back of one another's T-shirts or write a message, a favorite Scripture, or a slogan.

This activity can help unify your group and be used to launch a retreat, a mission trip, or a fun outing. From time to time, wear the T-shirts as a group and celebrate the spirit of unity.

Two-Hour Retreat—"A Great Cloud of Witnesses"

Big Idea: Build a retreat on the shoulders of faithful Christians

Key Bible Verses: Psalm 136; Hebrews 11:1–12:1 (NIV)

Supplies Needed: preferably a day with clouds, Bibles, concordances, pencils, paper, index cards, multiple pairs of binoculars, light snacks, soft drinks

Length: 2 hours

Age Level: high school

Don't despair if you find that a weekend retreat is out of your budget because of the costs of lodging, transportation, supplies, and food. All you need for this two-hour retreat is a shelter house, an outdoor gathering place, or maybe even a parked bus, and you can turn it into a retreat location without leaving town. This retreat works best on a day when there are plenty of clouds in the sky. Bring along a few helpers and volunteers, too, if you have a larger group.

Retreat Opening (45 minutes)
Gather the group, and open with a prayer or by having students talk about what God is doing in their lives. Afterward, divide the teenagers into groups of three or four, and give each group a pair of binoculars. Say something like: "I want you to take a few minutes to look up at the sky. You see all those clouds floating over us? In your group, I'd like you to identify as many different shapes, faces, and designs in those clouds. Be creative. Let your imagination take over. Once everyone is done, we'll all come back together and talk about what we saw."

Allow 15 minutes for cloud watching and then another five minutes for the groups to write down some of their findings on their index cards.

KEY

 Activity   Games   Support

 Camp/Retreats   Icebreaker    Teaching

 Food   Missions/Outreach   Worship

Bring everyone back together, and ask the teams to discuss their findings and observations with the larger group.

Ask the teenagers these questions:

- What were some of the common cloud shapes most of the groups observed today?

- How does cloud watching force you to use your imagination?

Retreat Lesson (1 hour)
Then give your teenagers a short break or provide a snack, and take a few minutes for a favorite group game (maybe one of the game ideas in this book).

Bring everyone back together after the game, and ask your students to return to the small groups from the cloud-watching activity. Say something like: "You've already taken time to look at the physical clouds floating over us. But have you ever thought about the idea of clouds spiritually? In your groups, you're going to take a few minutes to read Hebrews 11, a chapter in the New Testament that talks about men and women who had incredible faith and did incredible things for God. In the next chapter, the Bible talks about them as a great cloud (or crowd) of witnesses. That's pretty exciting and encouraging!"

Distribute the Bibles, concordances, pencils, and paper. Ask someone in each group to read aloud Hebrews 11, while the rest of the group makes a list of all the names mentioned in this passage.

Once the groups have compiled their lists, instruct them to use the concordances to find and discuss significant stories about two of these characters. For example, who was Moses, Rahab, or Gideon? Allow 20 minutes for this research and discovery.

Bring everyone back into a large group, and ask each small group to share one of the biblical stories about a hero of the faith. Allow 20 minutes for this activity.

After the groups have finished their presentations, ask these questions:

- Why do you think the writer of Hebrews used the phrase "cloud of witnesses" in Hebrews 12:1 to describe people who have kept the faith? (Note: The New Living Translation uses the phrase "crowd of witnesses," so some students may ask why their Bible doesn't use the word cloud. Both cloud and crowd communicate a similar concept of men and women who've gone ahead of us in honoring God with their lives.)

- Tell us one thing you find significant about one of the heroes that Hebrews mentions, and explain why it's significant.

- How were some of these people imperfect? What do their mistakes and sins tell you about the meaning of faith?

- Think about the people who have helped shape your life. Who would you include in your personal "great cloud of witnesses"? Tell us about them.

Allow 20 to 30 minutes for this discussion.

Retreat Closing (15 minutes)
Take one more break for a snack or a game of your choice. Allow about 10 minutes for this.

Bring the group together again for some final minutes of reflection and prayer, and close your retreat with Psalm 136 as a responsive reading, with the students saying "His faithful love endures forever" after each line you read.

KEY

  Activity Games Support

 Camp/Retreats Icebreaker Teaching

 Food Missions/Outreach Worship

Vacation Bible School—at Christmas (M)

Big Idea: Offer VBS during the holiday season

Supplies Needed: inexpensive or donated crafts, Bibles

Length: 1 day or 1 week

Age Level: high school

Many congregations offer dynamic summer outreach programs to children and families. But the Christmas season can also be an effective time for churches to minister to kids in their communities. Christmas is a festive time to help children discover the message of God's great love through a vacation Bible school experience.

Your youth ministry can be the primary source of volunteers for this effort, and if you want to get started, try conducting a one-day Christmastime Vacation Bible School to learn the ropes. Here's how:

- Open with all of the kids for a time of Christmas songs, skits, and festive décor.

- Conduct classes for the children, grouped together by age. Use Christmas-season curriculum that tells the story of Jesus in an age-appropriate way.

- Ask for donated craft materials or visit a dollar store to find a $5 bag of goodies.

- Play age-appropriate games.

- Close with a big gathering again and sing plenty of Christmas songs.

Once you've gotten comfortable with the one-day experience, your team may be ready to expand its efforts to an entire week. Use these same ideas as guidelines. Develop a theme or set of biblical characters for each day, and be sure to incorporate plenty of creativity and fun as you let younger kids discover the message of Christmas.

Wallet and Purse Ⓐ Ⓖ Ⓒ

Big Idea: Launch spontaneous fun with random stuff

Supplies Needed: wallets, purses

Age Level: high school

Looking for a quick, easy activity to take up some time while you're waiting at the airport, or while you're sitting in the church parking lot awaiting the chartered bus? Try one or two of these wallet and purse activities. Great fun.

Let's Make a Deal

You may remember the old Let's Make a Deal TV game show with Monty Hall. In that show, Hall would frequently give prizes to anyone who could pull out an unusual item from a wallet or purse.

Before your trip, fill a bag with inexpensive prizes. Then ask the teenagers to pull out their wallets and purses, and give prizes to the first person who can show you the following items:

- Postage stamp
- Photo of a parent
- Photo of a boyfriend or girlfriend
- Paper clip
- Pen or pencil
- Flash drive

- Piece of tape
- Library card
- Student pass
- Social Security card
- Birth certificate

Driver's License Comparison

This game may make a few people uncomfortable, but if you are looking for a laugh, invite your older teenagers to remove their driver's licenses from their wallets and purses. See who has the funniest photo, the most serious photo, the most glamorous photo, and the zaniest pose. This activity delivers great fun.

The Dollar Bill Game

This memory game involves cash—a favorite item for most teenagers! Pull out a $1 bill (or a $5, $10, or $20) and invite the teenagers to see how much they can remember about what's on the front and back of the various bills. For example, ask the teenagers what building is shown on the back of the $5 bill or how many times "10" appears on the back of a $10 bill. The more you study a bill, the more you'll discover all the intricate details on the currency. Give this one a try, and see if it doesn't challenge your own memory.

Photo Stories

Most people carry a few photos in their purses or wallets. Invite a teenager to remove one photo and then tell the group who is in the photo, and where and when the photo was taken. If there is a story connected to the photo (such as a vacation, a special event, or a meaningful moment), encourage the student to talk about that story, too. This one fits in well before "lights out" or roll call.

Numbers

Invite three teenagers to quickly recite their 10-digit home phone numbers (or a cell number) aloud. Then see if others in the group can reconstruct all three numbers from memory.

Weighing In

See which girl has the heaviest purse (carrying the most junk) and see which guy has the thickest wallet (needs a hip adjustment). It's a quick activity but good for a few laughs.

Wanted Posters (T)

Big Idea: Focus on how we are all "wanted" by God

Key Bible Verses: Romans 12:3

Supplies Needed: poster board, markers, instant camera or digital camera connected to a printer

Length: 45 minutes

Age Level: middle school or high school

Begin by taking a snapshot of everyone in the group. Each person should make a face that you might see on a "wanted poster" or a police mug shot. If you like, have some funny hats or makeup on hand to help the teenagers create their mug shots.

Once the instant pictures are developed—or after you've printed the photos on paper—allow each student to create a wanted poster for the group. This poster should contain some brief information about the individual (something the student would like the group to know) and a "reward" amount.

For example, here's the wanted poster text I've used for myself when our group has enjoyed this activity.

Wanted
For Preaching Mediocre Sermons
Todd "The Forked Tongue" Outcalt
Reward: $100,000
Last seen near Indianapolis
Married with two teenagers
A guy who enjoys kayaking and hiking
Can probably be picked up at a Dunkin' Donuts
Danger only to himself and his parishioners

KEY

 Activity

 Games

 Support

 **Camp/Retreats**

 Icebreaker

 Teaching

 Food

 **Missions/Outreach**

 Worship

Anyway, you get the "picture." The idea is to create a wanted poster that contains something personal and perhaps a tad self-incriminating.

After your teenagers have created their posters, read Romans 12:3 aloud. (This passage asks believers not to think of themselves more highly than they should, but to have sober judgment in all things—good teaching for anyone who might end up on a wanted poster.)

Then ask your teenagers these questions:

- How much do you think you are actually worth? (Remember your reward!)

- Why do we often struggle to develop and practice humility?

- Without humility, what kinds of problems might you encounter in life?

- What did this activity teach you about God's grace, forgiveness, and generosity?

Wash Those Toes

Big Idea: Experience a foot-washing ceremony

Key Bible Verses: John 13; Psalm 23

Supplies Needed: basin, water, towels, Bibles

Length: 30 minutes

Age Level: high school

Foot washing as modeled by Jesus in John 13 can be a meaningful and moving experience. A foot-washing ceremony can enhance a retreat or a camp, or it can draw your teenagers closer together during worship.

All you need are a simple large basin, a pitcher of water for pouring, and some bath towels. The person whose feet are being washed can sit behind the basin, while the one who is washing can kneel in front of the basin.

Here is a simple outline for a foot-washing experience.

Opening Prayer
Reading from John 13:1-17
Questions for Reflection or Discussion:

- What was Jesus attempting to communicate when he washed his disciples' feet?

- How is Jesus present when we wash each other's feet?

- Do you find it more difficult to serve or to be served? Why?

- Why does it feel so weird, difficult, or foreign for us to have someone wash our feet?

A Time of Testimony or Witness
Prayer
Foot Washing
Closing Prayer or Reading of Psalm 23

Water Games (G)

Big Idea: Play some simple games for just a few bucks

Supplies Needed: water hoses, buckets, sponges, squirt guns (depending on the specific game)

Age Level: middle school

During the summer months, play some inexpensive water games. Here are some options that require nothing more than water hoses, soaker sprayers, sponges, and some plastic. These great games will keep your teenagers cool on a hot day.

KEY

 (A) Activity

(G) Games

(S) Support

(C) Camp/Retreats

(I) Icebreaker

(T) Teaching

(F) Food

(M) Missions/Outreach

(W) Worship

The Gauntlet

Assemble an arsenal of Super Soakers or make your own by using well-rinsed plastic detergent bottles. Form lines along both sides of a sidewalk, and challenge each teenager to "run the gauntlet" through the middle of the Super Soaker lines. Everyone gets wet, and it's a fun game for a hot summer afternoon.

Sponge-Ball Squarepants

Soak several sponges inside a bucket of ice-cold water. Ask each teenager to find a partner. Play the traditional "egg toss" game using the ice-cold sponges instead of eggs. See which duo can get the farthest apart without dropping the sponge. On a hot day the sponges can be tough to catch, but they do provide refreshment.

Water Messages

If you have a large asphalt parking lot or a sidewalk near your church, try using a water hose to write messages on these surfaces. Don't open the hose fully—just a trickle of water works best. Challenge the teenagers to create water messages, artwork, or symbols on the asphalt or sidewalk. On a hot day it doesn't take long for the water to evaporate, and the group can try again if it doesn't go well the first time around.

Summer Slide

This one works well if you have a hillside that is within distance of a garden hose. Cover the hillside with a huge sheet of plastic, and then spray it down. This will create a slick surface. There's nothing fancy here—just a good summer sledding surface. The teenagers can slide down sitting, flopping, or on large sponges.

Wear Your Shoes Well (T)

Big Idea: Remember that God has uniquely created each of us

Key Bible Verses: Mark 1:16-20

Supplies Needed: Bible, shoes

Lesson Length: 40 minutes

Age Level: middle school or high school

This lesson works well for smaller groups. The group of teenagers should sit in a circle, with feet in the middle and the students facing each other. Ask the young people to remove their shoes and place them inside the circle. Then read Mark 1:16-20 aloud (Jesus' call to the fishermen from Galilee).

Then say something like: "Take a moment to look at the shoes in your circle. Try on another pair. Examine how other people's shoes may look newer or older or more worn than your own."

Ask these questions:

- What can we learn or discern about other people by looking at their shoes?

- Even if another person's shoes fit you, why don't they feel as comfortable as your own?

- Which is better, in your estimation—new shoes that have never been worn, or a pair of shoes that have been worn for some time? Why?

After this discussion, invite the teenagers to think about their own shoes. They do not need to answer aloud, but encourage them to think about the questions as you read each one.

KEY

 Activity

 Camp/Retreats

Food

Games

Icebreaker

Missions/Outreach

Support

Teaching

Worship

(If you believe your students will engage in honest conversation, go ahead and have them answer the questions aloud.)

Where have your shoes been in the past week? Where have they taken you?

- Have the places you've been and the sights you've seen consistently reflected your faith in Jesus? Why or why not?

- How have your feet followed Jesus in the past week? Where have you gone after faithfully responding to his call?

- Only you can fulfill the call of Christ in your life. You are the only one who can live your life! How do you feel realizing that no one can walk in your shoes or fill your shoes?

Close your lesson with a time of silence or by reading aloud this prayer:

"Gracious God, we give you thanks that you have made all things well. You have created us uniquely, too. And we thank you also for calling us to follow the Christ and to fish for people. Help us to walk this day and always in the faithful paths you have set for us. In his name we pray, amen."

What's the Point?

Big Idea: Survey your students on the purpose of worship

Supplies Needed: photocopies of the **"Worship and Me" handout (p. 176)**, pencils

Age Level: middle school or high school

Use this survey to get your students thinking about the purpose of worship, and along the way you may discover students who are passionate about using music as a tool for worshipping God during your youth services.

What's Your Job?

Big Idea: Seek God's guidance for a career

Key Bible Verses: Psalm 32:8; 1 Corinthians 12:4-6

Supplies Needed: Bibles, poster board, markers

Lesson Length: 30 minutes

Age Level: high school

Many older teenagers have taken the initial steps toward a thoughtful career path—whether that means leaving for college, heading into the military, or entering the workforce. But in difficult times, young people may feel unsure about what career to pursue. And others might benefit from some guidance as they consider what God has planned for their lives. This lesson can help teenagers consider their gifts, passions, and direction.

First, prepare four signs (poster board works well) that you can post on the four walls of the room where you meet. These signs should read:

Love It!   Not Sure   Hate It!   Don't Care

To begin the lesson, invite the teenagers to consider the questions:

- What am I passionate about?

- What motivates me?

- What type of work could I see myself doing for the next 20 or 30 years?

- How might God be involved in my work and life after high school?

KEY

 A Activity   **G** Games   **S** Support

C Camp/Retreats   **I** Icebreaker   **T** Teaching

F Food   **M** Missions/Outreach   **W** Worship

Say something like: "In just a moment, I'm going to begin reading a list of career ideas you might consider. After I read each one, reflect for a moment on how you feel about that possible career. Maybe you love it, you hate it, you aren't sure, or you don't care. Once you have an answer, run to the wall with the sign that most accurately reflects your response."

Teacher	Firefighter	Police officer
Soldier	Marriage counselor	Truck driver
Engineer	Psychologist	Business owner
Pastor	Actor/Actress	Hotel manager
Homemaker	Construction worker	Writer/Journalist
Mechanic	Artist	Sales person
Waitress	President	Computer programmer
Pharmacist	Veterinarian	Doctor
Writer	Geologist	Archaeologist
Farmer	Dancer	Business CEO

Following the reading of this list, invite the teenagers to sit on the floor in a circle. Ask:

- Did you see any pattern among the careers that you gave "love it" responses? What was the common thread?

- Which occupations were you most passionate about? Why do you think you felt that way?

- Which ones turned you off completely? Why do you think you responded that way?

- Which of the occupations surprised or piqued your interest?

- Do you think God cares about the specific career path you choose? Explain your answer.

Close by saying something like: "You'll face lots of options for the paths you choose in life—especially when it comes to your career. Psalm 32:8 tells us that God will instruct us and teach us in the way we should go. And in 1 Corinthians 12:4-6, we learn that God has gifted each of us. When it comes to a career, you're more likely to experience deep fulfillment and satisfaction when you pursue a path that blends your passions, your skills, and your spiritual gifts. Look for opportunities in that direction, and learn as much as you can about those careers. Then set your goals and strike out to accomplish them. God will guide you and help you along the path of your career and your life's calling."

Who Nose? (A)

Big Idea: Identify objects by their smell

Supplies Needed: blindfolds, an assortment of aromatic objects

Age Level: middle school or high school

Divide the youth group into teams if you would like to do this activity as a competition. Otherwise, just play for fun. Blindfold one teenager at a time, and hold an aromatic object under this person's nose. Give the teenager a few seconds to identify the object.

(Hint: The list is endless, but some of the objects that work well for this activity include a flower, onion, dirt, dog food, a piece of cheese, an orange, cologne, deodorant, ChapStick, and baby oil.)

KEY

 Activity   (G) Games   (S) Support

 (C) Camp/Retreats   (I) Icebreaker   (T) Teaching

 (F) Food   (M) Missions/Outreach   (W) Worship

Winter Games Ⓖ

Big Idea: Head outside for wintertime entertainment

Supplies Needed: old clothing, rope, sleds, marker flags (depending on the specific game)

Age Level: middle school or high school

If you live in a part of the country where you have to contend with the changing seasons, you'll find plenty of uses for some snow-covered game ideas. Try one of these to maximize a beautiful winter day.

Snowball Tag

Turn the traditional game of Tag into something chilling. "It" gets to toss snowballs. Anyone who gets hit is out. The last person remaining begins the next game as "It." Or don't even bother making anyone "It." Everyone gets two snowballs. People who are hit are out. Last person standing wins.

The Fling

Have your teenagers work together to fashion some high-caliber snowballs. Then see who can throw a snowball the farthest. Add a target to the mix, or see who can toss a snowball through a Hula Hoop or an old tire.

Snow-Crow

Bring in several pairs of old pants, some old flannel shirts, several lengths of rope, and some hats. Divide the teenagers into teams. Give each team a pair of pants, a shirt, and a hat. See which team can create the best "snow-crow" by stuffing the clothing with snow. Groups may use the rope to help secure the ends of the pants and the shirts and tie everything together. The snow-crows must be able to stand on their own.

Sledding Olympics

If your group has a favorite hill for sledding, round up a number of sleds and hold your own winter Olympics. Create a downhill course for tubing, make moguls, or fashion a slalom event using marker flags. Bring a stopwatch so you can keep the times. Organize individual medleys, relays, and team events. With a bit of ingenuity and creativity you should be able to conduct an entertaining athletic event for your teenagers.

Worship on the Mountain (W) (T)

Big Idea: Examine truths in the Sermon on the Mount

Key Bible Verses: Matthew 5–7

Supplies Needed: Bibles, newspapers, index cards, pencils, box

Length: 75 minutes   **Age Level:** high school

This worship experience, based on the Sermon on the Mount from Matthew 5–7, can be used in a variety of settings, including a retreat or camp.

Opening Prayer

God blesses those who are poor and realize their need for him, for the Kingdom of Heaven is theirs.

God blesses those who mourn, for they will be comforted.

God blesses those who are humble, for they will inherit the whole earth.

God blesses those who hunger and thirst for justice, for they will be satisfied.

God blesses those who are merciful, for they will be shown mercy.

KEY

 Activity   **Games**   **Support**

Camp/Retreats   **Icebreaker**   **Teaching**

Food   **Missions/Outreach**   **Worship**

God blesses those whose hearts are pure, for they will see God.

God blesses those who work for peace, for they will be called the children of God.

God blesses those who are persecuted for doing right, for the Kingdom of Heaven is theirs.

Singing (7 minutes)
Sing some favorite songs, hymns, or choruses.

Salt and Light (20 minutes)
For this portion of the worship experience, you will need your newspapers. Invite the teenagers to silently read sections of the newspaper while you read aloud Matthew 5:13-16.

Invite three to five people to share reflections based on the following questions:

- Find a news article that demonstrates the need for our saltiness in the world. What does it mean for you to be salt of the earth today?

- Find a news article that demonstrates the need for our light in this world. What does it mean for you to be light today?

Praying for Needs (20 minutes)
Have the kids reflect on Matthew 6:5-8 as you read the passage aloud.

Ask:

- What people need our prayers today?

- What situations need our prayers today?

- What others concerns must we take to God today in prayer?

Pray for the specific needs that your students identify. Close with a time of silent prayer, and then pray the Lord's Prayer together.

Singing (7 minutes)
Sing some favorite songs, hymns, or choruses.

Don't Worry, Don't Judge (20 minutes)

Read aloud Matthew 6:25–7:5. Then ask these questions:

- What do these verses teach you about worry? What principles from this passage can you put into practice this next week?

- Why do you think we are so quick to judge others before evaluating ourselves?

Close with a time of reflection. Distribute index cards and pencils, and ask students to write down personal worries on one side and ways we judge others on the other side. Place these cards in a box, and ask each teenager to commit these worries and judgments to God. Consider taking this box and burning or burying it as a reminder that God can help us change and start a new path in life.

Close with more singing, or use Matthew 7:24-27 as your closing prayer.

Wrap-a-Thon (S) (A)

Big Idea: Wrap up some quick funds during the Christmas season

Supplies Needed: wrapping paper, scissors, tape, ribbon

Age Level: middle school or high school

Many youth groups hold "wrap-a-thon" events during the Christmas season. This is usually a one-day event—typically just a morning or afternoon—where families can drop off their presents for wrapping. You'll need various colors and styles of wrapping paper, scissors, ribbon, and plenty of clear tape. Recruit a large crew of teenagers, parents, and adult volunteers for the event. You can request a donation of $1 or $2 for each

KEY

 Activity

 Camp/Retreats

 Food

 Games

 Icebreaker

 Missions/Outreach

 Support

Teaching

Worship

wrapped gift, or allow people to choose their own donation amount. With a few able hands, you can wrap up some quick funds with this idea.

Your Next Step ⓣ

Big Idea: Grow in your faith by taking risks

Key Bible Verses: Matthew 14:22-33

Supplies Needed: Bibles, blindfolds

Lesson Length: 25 minutes

Age Level: middle school or high school

Gather your teenagers, and have them stand in a large comfortable circle. Blindfold the participants—either all of your students or just a selected number to illustrate the big idea. Move them around to different parts of the room; you want them to feel uneasy or confused about exactly where they're standing and how easily they can move. Read aloud Matthew 14:22-33, the story of the stormy night at sea when both Jesus and Peter walked on the water. After the reading, invite those who are blindfolded to take a step of faith—just one step forward. Then ask them to take another. Then another.

Some of your teenagers will stop after one or two steps. Others will continue farther. After a few steps, remove the blindfolds. Then ask:

- How was the first step of faith different from the second step?

- What thoughts crossed your mind as you continued taking steps? (Or what caused you to stop walking?)

- What did you learn about yourself from this activity?

After discussing these ideas, invite your teenagers to think about the Bible passage you read. Ask these questions:

- Why do you think Peter sank?

- What is one thing you need to do soon that will involve faith, risk, or trust in Jesus to accomplish? Do you have more faith or more doubt right now? Explain your answer.

- How can you draw strength and confidence from Jesus during difficult times in your life? What are practical things you can do in these situations?

Close the lesson by praying that God would help each person in the group develop a deeper, stronger faith.

Your Story

Big Idea: Write brief biographies of people in your congregation

Supplies Needed: laptop computer, printer, small desk

Age Level: high school

Some years ago, I had a friend who made his living for a while by writing "one minute" stories on the street using a portable typewriter. He was fast and creative, and he was able to capture people's imaginations and their pocketbooks with the offer to write their stories.

You may not have someone in your group who is this fast and imaginative, but thanks to laptop computers, a writing project can be completed almost anywhere. Recruit some teenagers who either write well or listen well. Set up a small desk during some of your large church gatherings, invite people to tell their stories to this teenager, and you'll soon be publishing people's life stories. After your teenager completes the writing, invite people to make a donation to the youth ministry. This is a fun and meaningful idea that will help your teenagers connect with adults in your congregation.

KEY

Activity	Games	Support
Camp/Retreats	Icebreaker	Teaching
 Food	Missions/Outreach	Worship

Youth Devotional (W) (S)

Big Idea: Publish your teenagers' thoughts on living for God

Supplies Needed: paper, staples

Age Level: middle school or high school

Many churches publish annual Advent or Lenten devotionals with readings, reflections, and poems written by members of the congregation. Your youth ministry can also publish a devotional during these seasons or for special occasions such as retreats or mission trips. This devotional can add a personal dimension to your youth worship experience and can encourage teenagers to be more attentive in their personal prayers and reflections.

The devotional doesn't have to be large to be effective. And teenagers don't have to write long essays to make a point or share a testimony. Many will enjoy writing a poem or a paragraph on a theme.

During your youth meeting, distribute paper and pencils, and ask the teenagers to write down a reflection on any of the following:

- Event that shaped my life

- God-moment in my life

- Time when I felt God's strength or mercy

- Experience when I gave to someone in need

- One of the greatest joys I've ever experienced

Make copies of the devotional for distribution, or sell them as a fundraiser for a mission effort.

YouTube Worship Video (W)

Big Idea: Create a video that could rule the online world

Key Bible Verses: Psalm 146; Colossians 3:15-17

Supplies Needed: computer with Internet access

Age Level: high school

If you're looking for the latest viral video, you can probably find it on YouTube®. While a popular online destination for teenagers, YouTube® can also be a source of worship and outreach for your group. With just a little bit of creativity and time, your youth group can create a worship message, an original song, a video skit, or a reflection that can be posted on YouTube® for other teenagers to enjoy.

Here's a brief experience that might help prepare your teenagers before creating such a video. Gather together and select some favorite music (this could be on iPod, CD, or from the Internet). Read Colossians 3:15-17 aloud. Then ask:

- Think of specific times when you've been thankful to God. How did you show your thankfulness?

- What do you think verse 16 means by the phrase "spiritual songs"?

- Verse 17 says that in everything we say and do, we should remember that we are representatives of Jesus Christ. How does that principle affect our YouTube® project?

Gather around and give thanks. Close by praying Psalm 146 aloud.

Then head out to create your video!

KEY

(A) Activity   (G) Games   (S) Support

(C) Camp/Retreats   (I) Icebreaker   (T) Teaching

(F) Food   (M) Missions/Outreach   (W) Worship

Handouts

Can You Locate These?

1 Point	**2 Points**	**3 Points**
Guppy	Rawhide bone	Rose hair tarantula
Gerbil	Gerbil tube	Turtle food
Pug	Flea comb	Flax bird seed
Kitten	Green leash	Dog ID tag
Pigs ear	Cricket	Dog shampoo
Parakeet	Canned dog food	Turtle water dish
Gerbil Wheel	with gravy	Vegetarian cat
Book on dog training	Dog training DVD	Flea spray
Food	Worms	Cat magazine
Scorpion	Dog magazine	Parrot photo
Guinea Pig	Stuffed animal	Hairball medication
Ferret	Blue dog treat	Sack of fish food
Bird cage	Eel	

The Body, Mind, and Spirit Score Sheet

Using the point system below, keep a tally of your points during the challenge week. Individuals will total their points. A group's score will need to be averaged (total number of points divided by number of people in the group).

Body

- 2 points for every serving of fresh vegetables eaten
- 2 points for every serving of fresh fruit eaten
- 3 points for every day you don't eat fast food
- 3 points for drinking eight glasses of water per day
- 4 points for not smoking, drinking alcohol, or using tobacco products
- 4 points for exercising at least 15 minutes per day

Mind

- 2 points for completing all homework for that day
- 2 points for reading any additional material (novel, magazine, and so on)
- 3 points for completing a paper or project for school
- 3 points for having a deeper conversation with a teacher
- 4 points for each day you don't watch television
- 4 points for each day you don't surf the Internet, play video games, or use your iPod

Spirit

- 2 points for church attendance
- 2 points for youth group attendance
- 3 points for reading the Bible for 15 minutes or going to Bible study
- 3 points for praying at least 10 minutes per day
- 4 points for performing a random act of kindness
- 4 points for giving a tithe (10 percent of income) to God's work

Easter Narrative

Narrator 1: After the Sabbath, at dawn on the first day of the week, Mary Magdalene and the other Mary went to look at the tomb.

Narrator 2: There was a violent earthquake, for an angel of the Lord came down from heaven and, going to the tomb, rolled back the stone and sat on it. His appearance was like lightning, and his clothes were white as snow. The guards were so afraid of him that they shook and became like dead men. The angel said to the women:

Angel: Do not be afraid, for I know that you are looking for Jesus, who was crucified. He is not here; he has risen, just as he said. Come and see the place where he lay. Then go quickly and tell his disciples that he has risen from the dead and is going ahead of you into Galilee. There you will see him. Now I have told you.

Narrator 1: So the women hurried away from the tomb, afraid yet filled with joy, and ran to tell his disciples. Suddenly Jesus met them. As he greeted them, they clasped his feet and worshipped him. Jesus said:

Jesus: Greetings. Do not be afraid. Go and tell my brothers to go to Galilee; there they will see me.

Narrator 2: While the women were on their way, some of the guards went into the city and reported to the chief priests everything that had happened. When the chief priests had met with the elders and devised a plan, they gave the soldiers a large sum of money, telling them:

Priest: Just tell others that his disciples came during the night and stole him away while you were asleep. If this report gets to the governor, we will satisfy him and keep you out of trouble.

Narrator 1: So the soldiers took the money and did as they were instructed. Then the 11 disciples went to Galilee, to the mountain where Jesus had told them to go. When they saw him, they worshipped him; but some doubted. Then Jesus came to them and said:

Jesus: All authority in heaven and on earth has been given to me. Therefore go and make disciples of all nations, baptizing them in the name of the Father and the Son and the Holy Spirit and teaching them to obey everything that I have commanded you. And surely I am with you always, to the very end of the age.

The Exam

1. What is the greatest lesson you have learned as a teenager and why?

2. What was the greatest step of faith you took in high school?

3. What was the most important fact you have learned and why?

4. What was the most important thing you have learned about yourself during high school?

5. What was the most important thing you have learned about others?

6. What will be your creed for life and why?

7. What was the best thing you received from our youth group and why?

8. Who was your best teacher in high school and why?

9. How has your faith changed in high school?

10. How do you pray that your life will impact other people and why?

It's Optional!

Option 1
Select a favorite Bible story, find it in the Bible (get help if you need it), and then write a short profile about someone in the story. Here are some questions to think about as you write: Who is this person? What do you think this person looked like? What did you learn about this person's personality? How did God work in this person's life? What can I learn from this person's experiences? Be prepared to read your profile to your group.

Option 2
Fold this piece of paper like Origami to create a biblical, Christian, or personal symbol that is important to you. Go ahead and cut the paper if that helps you create your symbol. Be prepared to talk about the meaning of your symbol with the rest of the group.

Option 3
Pair up with another teenager for an interview. Ask whatever questions will help you learn more about the other person. Here are some possible questions, if you need help getting started: What's the best trip you've ever taken? How big is your family? What's the best movie you've ever seen? How has God worked in your life? Where do you hang out with friends? How do you spend your free time? What's your favorite verse in the Bible? What kind of job do you want when you're older? Take notes during your interview, and be prepared to introduce each other to the group.

Option 4
Write a poem that expresses how you feel about God, our church, or your life as a Christian. Your poem can rhyme, or it can be free verse. Use the back of this paper to write your poem. Read it to your group once everyone is finished.

Option 5
Walk around the room, and ask at least five people if they know of someone who needs prayer—a first name will do, and it can be a family member, acquaintance, or friend. Make a prayer list on the back of this paper, and be prepared to close our group session by leading a prayer for these individuals and their needs.

Step Out and Serve

Prayerfully give your thoughts on the following:

One mission opportunity that captures my heart is _____
_____
_____
_____

One mission project I would do for free is _____
_____
_____
_____

One nearby mission opportunity that could work well for our youth
group is _____
_____
_____

We can reach out to our community by _____
_____
_____
_____

One effective way to show our love to others is by _____
_____
_____
_____

I'm willing to help with _____
_____
_____
_____

Worship and Me

I define worship as _____
_____
_____
_____

The most important aspect of worship is _____
_____
_____
_____

The one thing that most effectively draws me into worship is _____
_____
_____

The most singable songs in our worship lineup are _____
_____
_____
_____

If we could add one thing to our worship services it would be_____
_____
_____
_____

I can help with our worship services by_____
_____
_____
_____

Appendix

Communicate Your Vision

I don't know the story of your youth ministry. Maybe you're experiencing tough times because your congregation has been hurt by a downturn in finances. Maybe your senior leadership has revised the budget, and your ministry took the first hit.

But this is one thing I do know from my experience as a youth pastor and a senior pastor: The more clearly you communicate your vision for ministering to the teenagers of your church and your community, the more likely your congregation will rally to support you and your efforts. Create a strong vision for your ministry and make sure you communicate it effectively with the church board or leadership.

How do you do this? Start by answering this set of questions. Better yet, walk through these questions with some of your adult leaders, student leaders, and key parents. Identify the vision, and then make the appeal.

- What is the purpose or mission of our youth ministry?

- What successes have we experienced in the past six months that demonstrate how God is working in the lives of our teenagers?

- How is our youth ministry complementing and fulfilling the larger purpose of our congregation through its focus on teenagers?

- If our youth ministry disappeared or diminished because of lack of funding support, how would this affect the rest of the congregation?

- What is our vision for our youth ministry for the next six months? For the next year? For the next five years?

A solid vision will give you a clearer sense of direction and purpose. This will help you talk directly to your key church leaders about the role of finances in creating and maintaining a healthy, vibrant youth ministry.

That vision also could open the door to these options, which could have long-term benefits for your youth ministry.

Planned Giving

Some of the people in your congregation might want to partner with the youth ministry through their estate planning. Even during a difficult financial season, some people might consider this type of special gift. Many people overlook the impact their gifts can have after their death, especially gifts of real estate, life insurance, or collectibles. Sharing this vision of the estate gift from time to time will help people remember the eternal impact they've had on the lives of others, and planned giving is a way that they can impact teenagers for decades to come.

The Youth Foundation

Consider establishing a youth endowment or foundation. Many people in your congregation would see the wisdom and value of helping to establish a long-term gift, and an endowment is a perfect vehicle for this type of giving. As the endowment grows, the youth ministry can accomplish some amazing work with these earnings.

Speak to a financial planner in your congregation or your community, and see if an endowment might be a long-term ministry vehicle. This could be an effective way to cast a large vision for the youth ministry that will help shape future generations.

Outside Grants

Grants can be a wonderful way to fund a new staff position, develop a ministry that will benefit a large number of young people, or add much-needed space to your youth facility. This fundraising or stewardship concept may be unfamiliar to many church leaders, but I've successfully written grants for many years. In fact, I've written grant proposals that have funded the church and some of our ministries with very significant monies. Here's how to get started.

Step One: See if you have a grant writer in your congregation. If you do, tap into this person's expertise.

Step Two: Identify one or two significant goals, plans, or projects for your youth group, and then couch a grant proposal around them. You'll need to be able to craft a storyline—this doesn't mean writing fiction, but offering a stirring narrative that relates your history, vision, and concepts related to how you would use the grant money.

Make this narrative passionate, accurate, and compelling.

Step Three: Craft an accurate budget for your proposal. For example, you'll need actual figures if you want to hire a new staff person (salary and benefits) or if you hope to expand your youth center (architectural design fees and construction costs). You will need to use this budget for future grant reports back to the foundation or granting entity. Keep good records and be specific.

Step Four: Articulate your timeline for the project. A grant cannot usually be open ended. There is a beginning and an end time frame.

Step Five: Submit your proposal. You'll need to locate foundations or trusts that work with churches or religious institutions—and you will likely need to present your proposal differently for each foundation. Locating a grant organization can intimidate most people, but here are some quick tips on how to do this, regardless of where you live.

- Begin searching online at grantstation.com. This online network will give you some quick hits and will help you locate foundations in your state or area.

- If you have money to invest in grant writing, check out the Foundation Center, foundationcenter.org. This online search engine is the best of its kind, and if you are successful at grant writing, this investment can pay for itself several times over. The Foundation Center also has books, CDs, and other resources that can assist you in your grant-writing endeavors.

- Check with other congregations that may have recently received grants.

- Check with nonprofit organizations that rely on grant money for their funding. They likely have many foundations and addresses.

- Check with large retailers like Target and Walmart. They usually have small community grants that churches can apply for—if you can, make a strong case that a ministry or program will benefit the whole community and not just your congregation.

- Don't overlook private family trusts and foundations. There are thousands of these around the country, and no matter where you live, there are probably a handful of private or family foundations nearby. Some of these smaller foundations, in fact, may actually give money specifically for mission and congregational needs. Many of these foundations were established because a family wanted to help build God's kingdom. The grants may not be as large, but many of these foundations love working with churches.

- Don't overlook matching grants from corporations. Some businesses will still match a contribution made by an employee, either dollar-for-dollar or using some other formula. Some of your church members may work for these companies. If you can find one or two people in your congregation who would donate $1,000 to the youth ministry, the company might match it. Does that stir your imagination?

If you are looking to write a grant, consider taking a grant-writing workshop. You'll discover the basics, and you'll be able to hone your skills and learn from those who are successful at the craft. Grant-writing is a skill that takes time and attention. Many large grants will demand a considerable outlay of time as you write the proposal, and some of these may almost constitute a book-length form by the time they are completed. But grants can considerably enhance the bottom line of a youth ministry's financial picture.

Many foundations provide matching grants. You may be required to have at least half the money on hand to apply for the match. But if you have access to these types of funds, a grant can get you over the top.

Finally, don't forget this: Foundations and endowments exist for the purpose of giving away money. They want to partner with other institutions and entities that will benefit the common good in some way. When fewer nonprofits and individuals apply for these grants due to tough times, these foundations are more eager to earmark a greater percentage of funds to successful applicants.

Recently, a friend of mine who works for a foundation told me that because they are receiving fewer grant proposals, they are eager to give more money to the smaller pool of applicants who are getting their names in the hat.

So if you have a vision, a dream, or a great idea for your youth ministry, don't just look to fund it through carwashes and bean dinners. Grant it!

Acknowledgements

The publication of this book is the work of many minds and hands, and I would like to thank the following people for making it possible.

I thank Rob Cunningham for serving as the head chef and for guiding this pot of ideas to its boiling point and to what, we hope, is a fine recipe for success and helpfulness in the world of youth ministry.

I thank Nadim Najm for adding many fine ingredients to the stew and for working on the recipe along with Rob.

I am also grateful to Rick Lawrence—who served in many capacities, including critic, host, and chef—and I also thank him now for working with me in the past and for giving me another opportunity to cook up a book.

Many thanks also to Andy Brazelton and Kerri Loesche. And, of course, I thank Thom and Joani Schultz for Group Publishing and all they do for youth leaders, pastors, and congregations everywhere.

My gratitude also goes out to the staff of Calvary United Methodist Church of Brownsburg, Indiana. I love you all, and I am blessed every day to work side by side with you in our little vineyard.

There are also scores of youth leaders, volunteers, and other miracle workers who have worked in the kitchen for decades, and I am grateful to every one who offered an idea, a spice, or a secret ingredient to the mix. I am always amazed at your creativity, resiliency, and resourcefulness as you minister to others.

Finally, I thank my wife, Becky, who had to watch the Food Network™ alone while I was writing this book. My son, Logan, also deserves thanks for being so agreeable with my soups, as does my daughter, Chelsey. Someday I'll cook up something more substantial and special for you all. But in the meantime, I hope my love will suffice.